AEROFILMS GUIDE

FOOTBALL GROUNDS

FOURTEENTH REVISED EDITION

AEROFILMS GUIDE

FOOTBALL GROUNDS

FOURTEENTH REVISED EDITION

Ian Allan
PUBLISHING

CONTENTS

CONTENTS

Front cover: **Undoubtedly the most dramatic wholly new league ground to have appeared in recent seasons is Arsenal's new Emirates Stadium with its 60,000 capacity. The ground saw its first game on 22 July 2006 when it played host to Dennis Bergkamp's testimonial.**

Preceding pages: **Manchester United's Old Trafford ground continues to grow ever larger; the new work has taken the stadium's capacity to an awesome 76,000. In London, however the even larger Wembley Stadium was hit by delays in construction, which meant that it was unavailable for fixtures during the 2005/06 season and the early qualifying matches for the 2008 European Championships will also not be played in London. Hopefully, the 2006/07 season will, however, see the long-running saga of the ground's reconstruction completed.**

First published in 1993;

Reprinted 1993 (twice); Second edition 1994; Third edition 1995; Fourth edition 1996; Fifth edition 1997; Sixth edition 1998; Seventh edition 1999; Eighth edition 2000; Ninth edition 2001; tenth edition 2002; 11th edition 2003, reprinted 2003. 12th edition 2004; 13th edition 2005; 14th Edition 2006.

ISBN (10) 0 7110 3127 4
ISBN (13) 978 0 7110 3127 2

Published by Ian Allan Publishing
an imprint of Ian Allan Publishing Ltd, Hersham, Surrey KT12 4RG.
Printed in England by Ian Allan Printing Ltd, Hersham, Surrey KT12 4RG

Code: 0608/G2

Text © Ian Allan Publishing Ltd 1993-2006
Diagrams © Ian Allan Publishing Ltd 2000-6
Aerial Photography © Simmons Aerofilms

Simmons Aerofilms Limited have been specialists in aerial photography since 1919. Their library of aerial photographs, both new and old, is in excess of 1.5 million images. Aerofilms undertake to commission oblique and vertical survey aerial photography, which is processed and printed in their specialised photographic laboratory. Digital photomaps are prepared using precision scanners.

Introduction

Welcome to the 14th edition of *Aerofilms Guide: Football Grounds*. By the time that this new edition hits the streets, the triumphs and tribulations of the 2005/06 season will have been long forgotten and the early season optimism that, somehow whatever happens, this will be the year for your team, will still be fresh. With the World Cup dominating the screens for much of the close season it is almost as though football has not been away, but the new campaign will be the focus of all our attentions for the next 10 months.

As is always the case, there are a number of new grounds featured in this year's edition. Two clubs — Arsenal and Doncaster Rovers — will either start the new season at a new venue or will move shortly after the start of the season. In terms of teams promoted from the Conference, we welcome back two names from the past: Hereford United and Accrington Stanley. In the case of the former, Edgar Street is still the club's venue and so this ground is restored to the league; in the case of Accrington, back after a gap of 44 years, the Fraser Eagle Stadium represents a new ground to the league as the club's original ground is no more. For other clubs — such as Milton Keynes Dons and Shrewsbury Town — the 2006/07 season represents the last campaign at their current homes; for the Dons, the National Hockey Stadium has been home for a relatively short period, but the Gay Meadow has been the Shrews' home for many years. One of your editor's favourite grounds, the loss of this picturesque ground located close to the River Severn in the town centre is particularly sad.

For this new edition, a number of further alterations have been included in terms of the factual information provided. This now includes a summary of last season's league form and also the club's nickname(s). it has also been decided to colour code each division; thus the Premier League is now gold; the League Championship is purple; League One is green; and League two is grey. It is hoped that these changes make the book more useful but, as always, any comments will be welcome. Please e-mail the editor at info@ianallanpublishing.co.uk

As always, the editorial team hope that you will have an enjoyable season and that your particular team achieves the success that you, as fans, think it deserves. Unfortunately, in any competition, there has to a winner, losers and the also-rans; we hope, whatever fate the season holds for your team, that you will make the most of the opportunities that the season offers.

Aerofilms

Aerofilms was founded in 1919 as Britain's first commercial aerial photography company and over the years its Library has grown to over 750,000 oblique aerial images, taken in black and white until the early 1980s, and colour from the early '70s to date. Amongst the unique photographs are aerial views of Crystal Palace before its destruction in 1937, and the airship R-101 on its maiden flight in 1929.

The Aerofilms Library also holds the negatives of Aero Pictorial Ltd (1934-60) and Airviews of Manchester (1947-92), which together number close to 200,000. In addition, there are smaller collections of ground photography, chiefly from postcard companies such as Stearns, Lilywhite, and Overland.

Aerofilms was a pioneer in the field of vertical or 'survey' photography and its capabilities in this field meant the company was co-opted into the war effort in 1940, forming part of the Photographic Development Unit. After the war the company concentrated on oblique aerial photography until 1987, when it took over the business of its sister company Hunting Surveys Ltd, which had specialised in vertical photography. As a result, Aerofilms' library of vertical photographs spans from the late 1940s to date, including county surveys and more specialised low-altitude surveys of coastlines and rivers.

Today forming part of the Blom group, a pan-European mapping company, Simmons Aerofilms has offices in Cheddar whilst its three aircraft fly from Cranfield Airport near Milton Keynes.

www.simmonsaerofilms.com

Disabled Facilities

We endeavour to list the facilities for disabled spectators at each ground. Readers will appreciate that these facilities can vary in number and quality and that, for most clubs, pre-booking is essential. Some clubs also have dedicated parking for disabled spectators; this again should be pre-booked if available.

MILLENNIUM STADIUM

Westgate Street, Cardiff CF10 1JA

Tel No: 0870 013 8600
Fax: 029 2023 2678
Stadium Tours: 029 208 22228
Web Site: www.millenniumstadium.com
E-Mail: info@cardiff-stadium.co.uk
Brief History: The stadium, built upon the site of the much-loved and historic Cardiff Arms Park, was opened in 2000 and cost in excess of £100 million (a tiny sum in comparison with the current forecast spend of over £600 million on the redevelopment of Wembley). As the national stadium for Wales, the ground will be primarily used in sporting terms by Rugby Union, but was used by the FA to host major fixtures (such as FA Cup and Carling Cup finals) until, in theory, 2006 when the new Wembley was scheduled for completion.

(Total) Current Capacity: 72,500
Nearest Railway Station: Cardiff Central
Parking (Car): Street parking only.
Parking (Coach/Bus): As directed by the police
Police Force and Tel No: South Wales (029 2022 2111)
Disabled Visitors' Facilities:
Wheelchairs: c250 designated seats. The whole stadium has been designed for ease of disabled access with lifts, etc.
Blind: Commentary available.
Anticipated Development(s): None planned

Above: 688019; Right: 687998

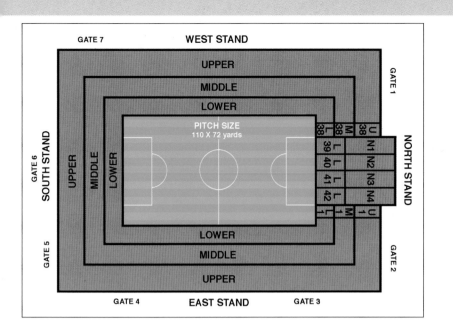

GATE 7   **WEST STAND**

UPPER

MIDDLE

LOWER

PITCH SIZE
110 X 72 yards

GATE 1

GATE 6
SOUTH STAND

UPPER

MIDDLE

LOWER

LOWER

MIDDLE

UPPER

NORTH STAND

U 38	38 M	L 38
N1	L 39	
N2	L 40	
N3	L 41	
N4	L 42	
U 1	M 1	L 1

GATE 2

GATE 5

GATE 4   **EAST STAND**   GATE 3

Fraser Eagle Stadium, Livingstone Road, Accrington, Lancashire BB5 5BX

Telephone: 01254 356950
Advance Tickets Tel No: 01254 356950
Fax: 01254 356951
Web Site: www.accringtonstanley.co.uk
E-mail: info@accringtonstanley.co.uk
League: League Two
Last Season: 1st (promoted from the Conference) (P 42; W 28; D 7; L 7; GF 76; GA 45)
Nickname: The Reds, Stanley
Nicknames: Stanley; The Reds
Brief History: The original club was formed as Accrington Villa in 1891 becoming Accrington Stanley in 1895. The team entered the Football League in 1921 and remained a member until its resignation in 1962. Following four years outside the League, the original club folded in 1966 and was not resurrected until 1970. The club has been based at the Crown Ground (now called the Fraser Eagle stadium) since it was reformed but prior to 1966 the original club played at Peel Park, which is now demolished. Record

Attendance (at Fraser Eagle Stadium) 4,368
(Total) Current Capacity: 5,057 (1,200 seated)
Visiting Supporters' Allocation: 400-1,500 max (in Coppice Terrace — open)
Club Colours: Red shirts and white shorts
Nearest Railway Station: Accrington (20min walk)
Parking (Car): Free places at ground located behind both goals; on-street parking in vicinity of ground
Parking (Coach/Bus): As directed
Police Force and Tel No: Lancashire Police (01254 382141)
Disabled Visitors' Facilities:
 Wheelchairs; Available
 Blind: No special facility
Anticipated Development(s):

KEY

⬆ North direction (approx)

❶ A680 Whalley Road
❷ To town centre and Accrington BR station (one mile)
❸ Livingstone Road
❹ Cleveleys Road
❺ Coppice Terrace (away)

Above: 700440; *Right:* 700450

Some 44 years after Accrington Stanley resigned from the Football League and after many years of the club gradually ascending through the non-league structure after its renaissance, Stanley were promoted back to the Football League as champions of the Conference. Under John Coleman, who has been the team's manager since 1999, Stanley were a dominant force in the Conference throughout the campaign, with promotion being assured well before the end of the season. One of the great ironies with the 2005/06 season was that, when Stanley resigned in 1962, the club that was elected in their place was Oxford United; however, at the end of the season, Oxford United were relegated to the Conference as a result of defeat on the final day by Leyton Orient. The rise of Stanley was aided by money from the sale of Brett Ormerod from Blackpool to Southampton; at this higher level the windfall may not be as significant a factor as it was in the Conference but the club should still make an impact at this level as other promoted clubs have done in the past. Provided that the team makes a reasonable start to the 2006/07 season, a top-half finish should not be beyond possibility but perhaps a season of consolidation might not be a bad thing.

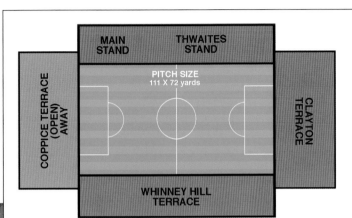

Emirates Stadium, London

Telephone: 020 7704 4000
Advance Tickets Tel No: 020 7704 4040
Fax: 020 7704 4001
Web Site: www.arsenal.com
E-mail: info@arsenal.co.uk
League: F.A. Premier
Last Season: 4th (P 38; W 20; D 7; L 11; GF 68; GA 31)
Nickname: The Gunners
Brief History: Founded 1886 as Royal Arsenal, changed to Woolwich Arsenal in 1891 and Arsenal in 1914. Former grounds: Plumstead Common, Sportsman Ground, Manor Ground (twice), moved to Arsenal Stadium in 1913 and to new Emirates Stadium for start of the 2006/07 season. Record attendance (at Highbury) 73,295
(Total) Current Capacity: 60,000
Visiting Supporters' Allocation: 3,000 (South East Corner)
Club Colours: Red and white shirts, white shorts

Nearest Railway Station: Finsbury Park or Drayton Park (Network Rail); Arsenal and Holloway Road (Underground)
Parking (Car): Residents' only parking scheme with special permits in the streets surrounding the ground and local road closures on matchdays
Parking (Coach/Bus): Queensland Road and Sobell Centre car park or as directed by the police
Police Force and Tel No: Metropolitan (020 7263 9090)
Disabled Visitors' Facilities:
  Wheelchairs: tbc
  Blind: tbc
Anticipated Development(s): The club moves into the new Emirates Stadium for the start of the 2006/07 season, leaving Highbury, its home for the past 93 years, to be redeveloped as apartments although the work will incorporate the listed structures at the ground.

KEY

↑ North direction (approx)

❶ North Bridge
❷ South Bridge
❸ Drayton Park Station
❹ Drayton Park
❺ East Coast Main Line
❻ To Finsbury Park Station
❼ To Arsenal Underground Station
❽ South East Corner (away)

Above: 700190; *Right:* 700183

In the Gunners' final season at Highbury the club could have been regarded as a team in transition in more than one way. It was the end of an era for the old stadium when Arsenal defeated Wigan 4-2 in the final game ever to be played at the venerable ground but there was also an air that the generation of players that had brought the team much domestic success over the past decade — Dennis Bergkamp, Robert Pires and Ashley Cole had also played their last domestic game for the Gunners. Domestically, the 2005/06 season was not one of the greatest in Arsenal's history as the team struggled, particularly away from home, in the Premier League and, indeed, snatched the all-important fourth place from rivals Tottenham only on the last Sunday of the season when victory over Wigan combined with Spurs' defeat at West Ham ensured that the team would again feature in the Champions League. It was in the Champions League that the club achieved some of its greatest performances, reaching the final after strong performances against fancied teams in the knock-out phase. Against Barcelona, however, in the final, playing for more than 70 minutes with ten men after Jens Lehmann's sending off — the first ever in a Champions League final — the Gunners were unlucky to lose 2-1 after having taken an unlikely lead. With players such as Eboue, Fabregas, Toure and Reyes all now showing their considerable talent, Arsene Wenger's team should certainly be a force again in the Premier League in 2006/07.

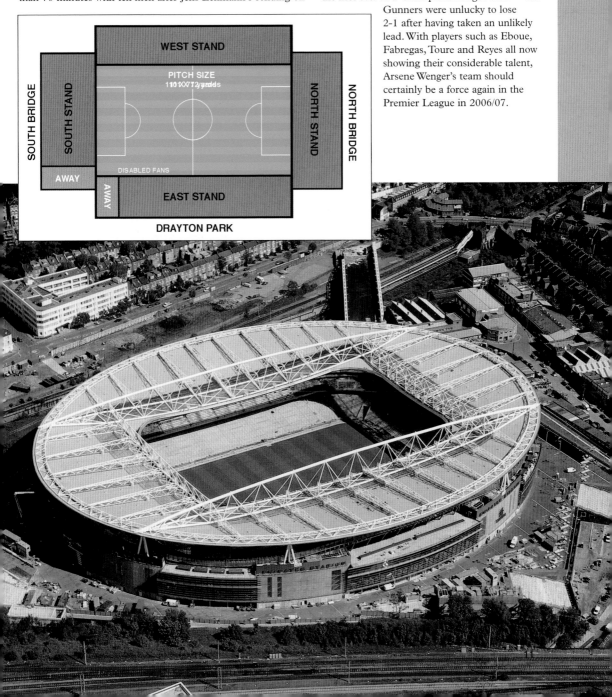

WEST STAND

PITCH SIZE
110 X 72 yards

SOUTH BRIDGE

SOUTH STAND

NORTH STAND

NORTH BRIDGE

DISABLED FANS

AWAY

AWAY

EAST STAND

DRAYTON PARK

Villa Park, Trinity Road, Birmingham, B6 6HE

Tel No: 0121 327 2299
Advance Tickets Tel No: 0121 327 5353
Fax: 0121 322 2107
Web Site: www.avfc.premiumtv.co.uk
E-Mail: commercial.dept@astonvilla-fc.co.uk
League: F.A. Premier
Last Season: 16th (P 38; W 10; D 12; L 16; GF 42; GA 54)
Nickname: The Villans
Brief History: Founded in 1874. Founder Members Football League (1888). Former Grounds: Aston Park and Lower Aston Grounds and Perry Barr, moved to Villa Park (a development of the Lower Aston Grounds) in 1897. Record attendance 76,588
(Total) Current Capacity: 42,573 (all seated)
Visiting Supporters' Allocation: Approx 2,983 in North Stand

Club Colours: Claret and blue shirts, white shorts
Nearest Railway Station: Witton
Parking (Car): Asda car park, Aston Hall Road
Parking (Coach/Bus): Asda car park, Aston Hall Road (special coach park for visiting supporters situated in Witton Lane)
Police Force and Tel No: West Midlands (0121 322 6010)
Disabled Visitors' Facilities:
  Wheelchairs: Trinity Road Stand section
  Blind: Commentary by arrangement
Anticipated Development(s): In order to increase the ground's capacity to 51,000 Planning Permission has been obtained to extend the North Stand with two corner in-fills. There is, however, no confirmed timescale for the work to be completed.

KEY

C Club Offices
S Club Shop
E Entrance(s) for visiting supporters
R Refreshment bars for visiting supporters
T Toilets for visiting supporters

↑ North direction (approx)

❶ B4137 Witton Lane
❷ B4140 Witton Road
❸ Trinity Road
❹ To A4040 Aston Lane to A34 Walsall Road
❺ To Aston Expressway & M6
❻ Holte End
❼ Visitors' Car Park
❽ Witton railway station
❾ North Stand
❿ Trinity Road Stand

ASTON VILLA

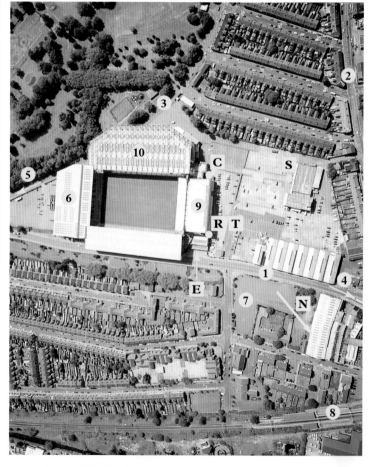

Above: 697435; Right: 697425

In a dire season for football in Birmingham, Villa can at least claim to have won the local title for the highest placed team from the West Midlands in the Premier League although, given that both City and the Baggies were relegated, that is not a particularly onerous position to have achieved. Whilst never looking as though they were going to get dragged into the relegation mire, David O'Leary's players performed only in fits and starts and in previous seasons, teams with more than 40 points have been relegated. There were occasional bright spots, such as the 4-0 victory away at Middlesbrough, but these were too few to prevent increasing disquiet around the ground both over O'Leary and over chairman Doug Ellis. Whatever happens during the close season, it's likely that there will be a clear out of many of the under-performing players — indeed the now departed O'Leary had been told that he must make cuts before he could bring in fresh talent — and a number of new faces will undoubtedly feature in 2006/07. With three relatively weak teams being promoted in 2005/06, there should be no threat to Villa's Premier League position during 2006/07.

Away from the league, Villa were involved in a game that led to one of the strangest scores of the season, when they defeated Wycombe Wanderers 8-3 away in the second round of the Carling Cup, having been 3-1 down at half time although this was followed by an embarrassing 3-0 defeat at League One Doncaster.

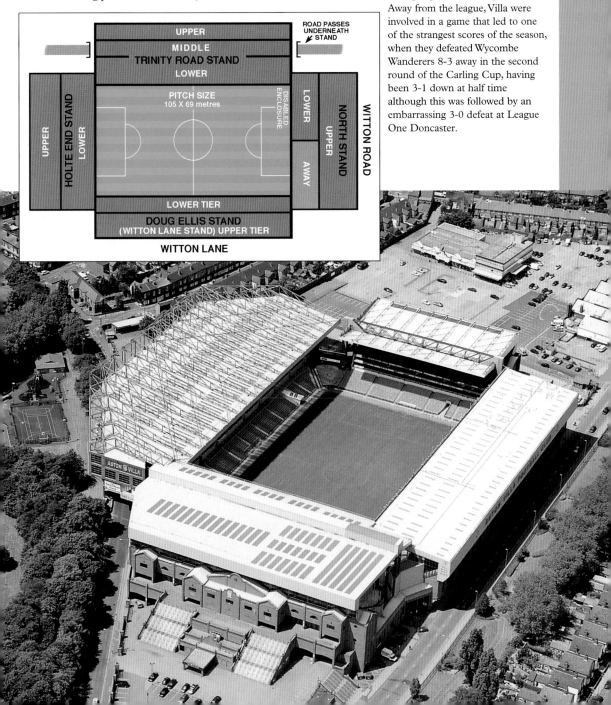

Underhill Stadium, Barnet Lane, Barnet, Herts EN5 2DN

Telephone: 020 8441 6932
Advance Tickets Tel No: 020 8449 6325
Fax: 020 8447 0655
Web site: www.barnetfc.premiumtv.co.uk
E-mail: info@barnetfc.com
League: League Two
Last Season: 18th (P 46; W 12; D 17; L 17; GF 44; GA 57)
Nickname: The Bees
Brief History: Founded 1888 as Barnet Alston. Changed name to Barnet (1919). Former grounds: Queens Road and Totteridge Lane; moved to Underhill in 1906. Promoted to Football League 1991; relegated to Conference 2001; promoted to League 2 2005. Record attendance, 11,026
(Total) Current Capacity: 5,500
Visiting Supporters' Allocation: 1,000 on South Stand (open) plus 500 on East Terrace is required.
Colours: Black and gold shirts, black shorts
Nearest Railway Station: New Barnet (High Barnet — Tube)

Parking (Car): Street Parking and High Barnet station
Parking (Coach/Bus): As directed by police
Police Force and Tel No: Metropolitan (020 8200 2112)
Disabled Visitors' Facilities:
  Wheelchairs: 12 positions on east side of North Terrace
  Blind: No special facility
Anticipated Development(s): The club's long-term ambition remains to relocate from Underhill and announced that, in the event of being unable to locate a suitable site within the borough, it would look outside Barnet provided that any new site was within a 'reasonable travelling distance' of the existing ground. Of more immediate concern was a dispute with the local council over vehicular access to the ground; this was resolved in late May with a 12-month extension granted by the council for the use of Priory Road. Without this, Underhill would not have met Football League ground criteria.

KEY

C Club Offices
S Club Shop
E Entrance(s) for visiting supporters
R Refreshment bars for visiting supporters
T Toilets for visiting supporters

↑ North direction (approx)

❶ Barnet Lane
❷ Westcombe Drive
❸ A1000 Barnet Hill
❹ New Barnet BR station (one mile)
❺ To High Barnet tube station, M1 and M25
❻ Holte End

BARNET

Above: 699356; *Right:* 699359

Promoted from the Conference at the end of the 2004/05 season, it looked for part of the season as though the Bees were going to make an immediate return to the Conference as the team hovered just above the drop zone. However, Paul Fairclough's team did just enough to finish in 18th place, some five points above relegated Oxford United. Away from the league, the club had a storming 4-2 victory in the Carling Cup at League One Bristol City and an equally impressive 2-1 victory at Underhill over Plymouth in the second. One cause of concern for the future, however, is the team's lack of prowess up front; scoring only 44 goals during the league season was amongst the worst performances in the division and strengthening this area will be one of Fairclough's priorities during the close season. Provided that the club can recruit then again a position above the drop zone beckons; otherwise the club could well struggle to retain its League status in 2006/07.

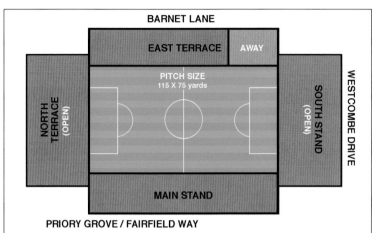

Oakwell Stadium, Grove Street, Barnsley, S71 1ET

Tel No: 01226 211211
Advance Tickets Tel No: 01226 211200
Fax: 01226 211444
Web Site: www.barnsleyfc.premiumtv.co.uk
E-mail: marketing@barnsleyfc.co.uk
League: League Championshi;
Last Season: 5th(promoted) (P 46; W 18; D 18; L 10; GF 62; GA 44)
Nickname: The Tykes
Brief History: Founded in 1887 as Barnsley St Peter's, changed name to Barnsley in 1897. Former Ground: Doncaster Road, Worsboro Bridge until 1888. Record attendance 40,255
(Total) Current Capacity: 23,009 (all seated)
Visiting Supporters' Allocation: 6,000 maximum (all seated; North Stand)

Club Colours: Red shirts, white shorts
Nearest Railway Station: Barnsley
Parking (Car): Queen's Ground car park
Parking (Coach/Bus): Queen's Ground car park
Police Force and Tel No: South Yorkshire (01266 206161)
Disabled Visitors' Facilities:
  Wheelchairs: Purpose built disabled stand
  Blind: Commentary available
Future Development(s): With the completion of the new North Stand with its 6,000 capacity, the next phase for the redevelopment of Oakwell will feature the old West Stand with its remaining open seating. There is, however, no timescale for this work.

KEY
C Club Offices
S Club Shop
E Entrance(s) for visiting supporters

↑ North direction (approx)

❶ A628 Pontefract Road
❷ To Barnsley Exchange BR station and M1 Junction 37 (two miles)
❸ Queen's Ground Car Park
❹ North Stand
❺ Grove Street
❻ To Town Centre

Above: 697496; *Right:* 697497

One of the teams in the chasing pack for the automatic promotion spot, Barnsley were never quite good enough to threaten one of the top two positions, unlike Brentford, Huddersfield and Swansea, but ultimately were to have the final laugh over their Play-Off rivals. However, it was not until the final weekend of the season that Andy Ritchie's team secured a top six finish as victory away at relegated Walsall ensured that a Play-off berth was assured irrespective of events at Bradford (where Nottingham Forest needed a win) or Tranmere (where Doncaster also needed victory). In the Play-Off semi-final, Barnsley faced much fancied Huddersfield Town and all seemed lost when the team faced a 1-0 defeat at home. A stunning victory at Huddersfield, however, meant that the team faced a trip to the Millennium Stadium with a final against Swansea. With the score 2-2 after extra time, penalties resulted and Barnsley's nerve proved stronger. Thus League Championship football will be on offer at Oakwell in 2006/07; as a promoted team, particularly through the Play-Offs, Barnsley will undoubtedly be a favourite for the drop, but under Ritchie's astute management the team should have the potential to consolidate itself at this higher level.

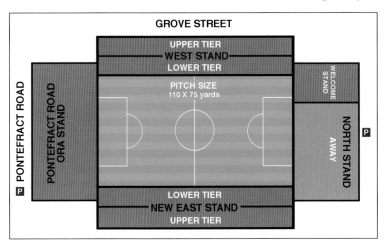

St Andrew's Stadium, St Andrew's Street, Birmingham, B9 4NH

Tel No: 0871 226 1875
Advance Tickets Tel No: 0871 226 1875
Fax: 0121 772 5715
Web Site: www.bcfc.premiumtv.co.uk
E-Mail: reception@bcfc.com
League: League Championship
Last Season: 18th (relegated) (P 38; W 8; D 10; L 20; GF 28; GA 41)
Nickname: The Blues
Brief History: Founded 1875, as Small Heath Alliance. Changed to Small Heath in 1888, Birmingham in 1905, Birmingham City in 1945. Former Grounds: Arthur Street, Ladypool Road, Muntz Street, moved to St Andrew's in 1906. Record attendance 66,844
(Total) Current Capacity: 30,016 (all seated)
Visiting Supporters' Allocation: 3-4,500 in new Railway End (Lower Tier)
Club Colours: Blue shirts, white shorts

Nearest Railway Station: Bordesley
Parking (Car): Street parking
Parking (Coach/Bus): Coventry Road
Police Force and Tel No: West Midlands (0121 772 1169)
Disabled Visitors' Facilities:
  Wheelchairs: 90 places; advanced notice required
  Blind: Commentary available
Future Development(s): The proposals for the Digbeth ground have not progressed and any future development is likely to involve work at St Andrews, where there are plans for the possible redevelopment of the Main Stand to take the ground's capacity to 36,500. There is no timescale for the £12 million project and with the club's relegation from the Premier League every possibility that it will be deferred.

KEY

- **C** Club Offices
- **S** Club Shop
- **E** Entrance(s) for visiting supporters

⬆ North direction (approx)

- ❶ Car Park
- ❷ B4128 Cattell Road
- ❸ Tilton Road
- ❹ Garrison Lane
- ❺ To A4540 & A38 (M)
- ❻ To City Centre and New Street BR Station (1½ miles)
- ❼ Railway End
- ❽ Tilton Road End
- ❾ Main Stand
- ❿ Kop Stand
- ⓫ Emmeline Street
- ⓬ Kingston Road
- ⓭ St Andrew's Street

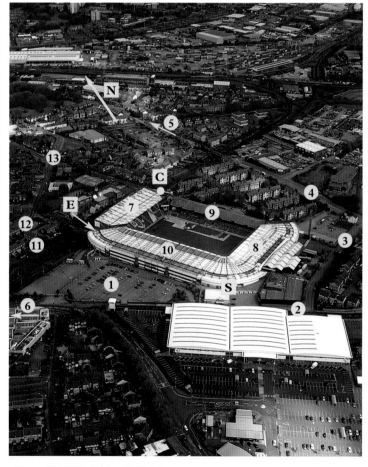

Above: 699252; Right: 699246

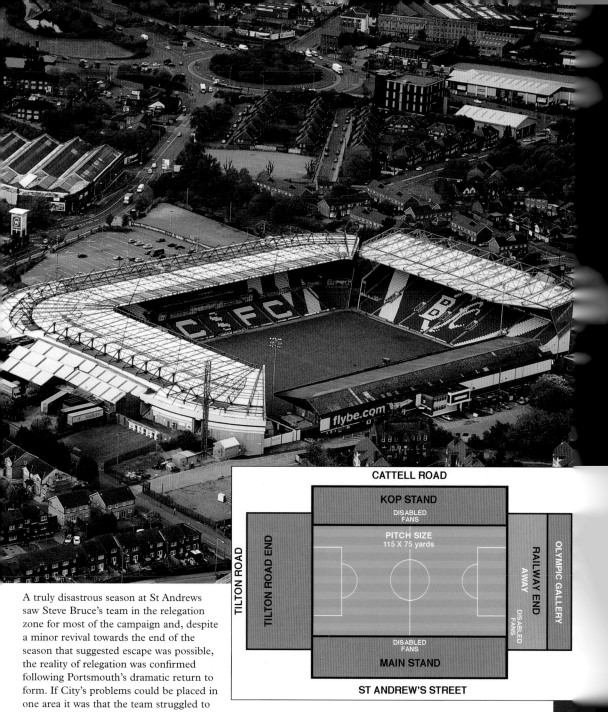

CATTELL ROAD

KOP STAND

DISABLED FANS

PITCH SIZE
115 X 75 yards

TILTON ROAD

TILTON ROAD END

RAILWAY END AWAY

DISABLED FANS

OLYMPIC GALLERY

DISABLED FANS

MAIN STAND

ST ANDREW'S STREET

A truly disastrous season at St Andrews saw Steve Bruce's team in the relegation zone for most of the campaign and, despite a minor revival towards the end of the season that suggested escape was possible, the reality of relegation was confirmed following Portsmouth's dramatic return to form. If City's problems could be placed in one area it was that the team struggled to score goals all season; the tally of 28 league goals was one of the lowest in the Premier League. If ever the cliché about goals winning games was appropriate it was at St Andrews in 2005/06. On paper — with strikers such as Emile Heskey, Mikael Forsell and, later, Chris Sutton available — goals should not have been City's problem, but Bruce was unlucky with injuries and this undoubtedly was significant in the club's loss of confidence and its Premier League place. After some uncertainty, it was confirmed that Bruce would retain his position for the League Championship and, as one of the relegated teams, City will certainly be amongst the favourites for an immediate return. Defensively, City look strong; provided that the frailties up-front can be addressed then Bruce's team should certainly feature in the promotion hunt. However, as Norwich, Southampton and Palace discovered in 2005/06, the Championship can be a graveyard for clubs with Premier League ambitions following relegation.

Ewood Park, Blackburn, Lancashire, BB2 4JF

Tel No: 08701 113232
Advance Tickets Tel No: 08701 123456
Fax: 01254 671042
Web Site: www.rovers.premiumtv.co.uk
E-Mail: commercial@rovers.co.uk
League: FA Premier
Last Season: 6th (P 38; W 19; D 6; L 13; GF 51; GA 42)
Nickname: Rovers
Brief History: Founded 1875. Former Grounds: Oozebooth, Pleasington Cricket Ground, Alexandra Meadows. Moved to Ewood Park in 1890. Founder members of Football League (1888). Record attendance 61,783
(Total) Current Capacity: 31,367 (all seated)
Visiting Supporters' Allocation: 3,914 at the Darwen End

Club Colours: Blue and white halved shirts, white shorts
Nearest Railway Station: Blackburn
Parking (Car): Street parking and c800 spaces at ground
Parking (Coach/Bus): As directed by Police
Police Force and Tel No: Lancashire (01254 51212)
Disabled Visitors' Facilities:
  Wheelchairs: All sides of the ground
  Blind: Commentary available
Anticipated Development(s): There remain plans to redevelop the Riverside (Walker Steel) Stand to take Ewood Park's capacity to c40,000, but there is no confirmation as to if and when this work will be undertaken.

KEY

C Club Offices
S Club Shop
E Entrance(s) for visiting supporters
R Refreshment bars for visiting supporters
T Toilets for visiting supporters

⬆ North direction (approx)

❶ A666 Bolton Road
❷ Kidder Street
❸ Nuttall Street
❹ Town Centre & Blackburn Central BR station (1½ miles)
❺ To Darwen and Bolton
❻ Darwen End
❼ Car Parks
❽ Top O'Croft Road

Above: 698991; *Right:* 698999

BLACKBURN ROVERS

Under Mark Hughes, Rovers had a much improved season in 2005/06; whilst never threatening the dominance of the top two teams, the club was in the hunt for the all-important fourth position until virtually the end of the campaign. Finishing sixth brings European football again to Ewood Park, courtesy of the UEFA Cup, and it is perhaps in the cup competitions that Rovers' best chance of glory comes. With four or five teams now in a position to dominate the top-four places, Rovers undoubtedly has the capability to again be in the hunt for the UEFA Cup spots at the end of the 2006/07 season but probably fifth or sixth is the best that the team can hope for.

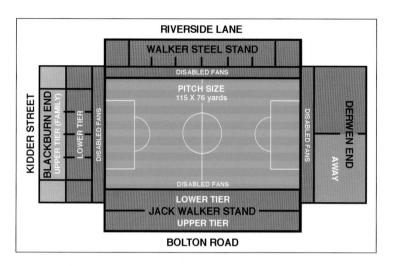

RIVERSIDE LANE

WALKER STEEL STAND

DISABLED FANS

PITCH SIZE
115 X 76 yards

KIDDER STREET

BLACKBURN END

UPPER TIER (FAMILY)

LOWER TIER

DISABLED FANS

DISABLED FANS

DERWEN END

AWAY

DISABLED FANS

LOWER TIER
JACK WALKER STAND
UPPER TIER

BOLTON ROAD

Seasiders Way, Blackpool, Lancashire, FY1 6JJ

Tel No: 0870 443 1953
Advance Tickets Tel No: 0870 443 1953
Fax: 01253 405011
E-Mail: info@blackpoolfc.co.uk
Web Site: www.blackpoolfcpremiumtv.co.uk
League: League One
Last Season: 19th (P 46; W 12; D 17; L 17; GF 56; GA 64)
Nickname: The Seasiders
Brief History: Founded 1887, merged with 'South Shore' (1899). Former grounds: Raikes Hall (twice) and Athletic Grounds, Stanley Park, South Shore played at Cow Cap Lane, moved to Bloomfield Road in 1899. Record attendance 38,098
(Total) Current Capacity: 9,000 (all seated)
Visiting Supporters' Allocation: 1,700 (all seated) in East Stand (open)

Club Colours: Tangerine shirts, white shorts
Nearest Railway Station: Blackpool South
Parking (Car): At Ground and street parking (also behind West Stand – from M55)
Parking (Coach/Bus): Mecca car park (behind North End (also behind West Stand – from M55)
Other Club Sharing Ground: Blackpool Panthers RLFC
Police Force and Tel No: Lancashire (01253 293933)
Disabled Visitors' Facilities:
   Wheelchairs: North and West stands
   Blind: Commentary available (limited numbers)
Anticipated Development(s): The go-ahead has been given for the construction of a new £2 million South Stand. Once completed, this will add 2,000 seats to the ground's capacity although there is as yet no schedule for the work.

KEY

↑ North direction (approx)

❶ Car Park
❷ To Blackpool South BR Station (1½ miles) and M55 Junction 4
❸ Bloomfield Road
❹ Central Drive
❺ Henry Street
❻ East Stand (away)
❼ Site of South Stand
❽ West (Pricebusters Matthews) Stand
❾ North Stand

BLACKPOOL

Above: 699043; *Right:* 699048

With the Seasiders languishing at the wrong end of League One, manager Colin Hendry was sidelined after almost 18 months in the job in mid-November — although he had seen the club defeat Championship outfit Hull City 2-1 in the first round of the Carling Cup earlier in the season — and later in the month departed from the club. His position was taken, initially on a caretaker basis but then confirmed until the end of the season, by Simon Grayson, under whose auspices the team achieved a good 5-2 victory in its first match. Under Grayson, the club survived — just — in League One, finishing in 19th position some three points above relegated Hartlepool. Just after the end of the season it was confirmed that a Latvian businessman, Valeri Belokon, was intending to invest some £5 million in the club over the next few seasons. With this additional funding available, Grayson should have the opportunity of strengthening the squad and, if he achieves this, then Blackpool should have the potential to make the Play-Offs at least in a division where the acquisition of a couple of quality players can make a huge difference.

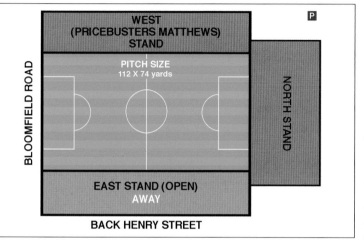

Reebok Stadium, Burnden Way, Lostock, Bolton, BL6 6JW

Tel No: 01204 673673
Advance Tickets Tel No: 0871 871 2932
Fax: 01204 673773
E-Mail: reception@bwfc.co.uk
Web Site: www.bwfc.premiumtv.co.uk
League: FA Premier
Last Season: 8th (P 38; W 15; D 11; L 12; GF 49; GA 41)
Nickname: The Trotters
Brief History: Founded 1874 as Christ Church; name changed 1877. Former grounds: Several Fields, Pikes Lane (1880-95) and Burnden Park (1895-1997). Moved to Reebok Stadium for 1997/98 season. Record attendance (Burnden Park): 69,912. Record attendance of 28,353 at Reebok Stadium
(Total) Current Capacity: 28,723 (all-seater)

Visiting Supporters' Allocation: 5,200 maximum (South Stand)
Club Colours: White shirts, white shorts
Nearest Railway Station: Horwich Parkway
Parking (Car): 2,800 places at ground with up 3,000 others in proximity
Parking (Coach/Bus): As directed
Police Force and Tel No: Greater Manchester (01204 522466)
Disabled Visitors' Facilities:
  Wheelchairs: c100 places around the ground
  Blind: Commentary available
Anticipated Developments(s): The station at Horwich Parkway has now opened. There are currently no further plans for the development of the Reebok Stadium.

BOLTON WANDERERS

KEY

↑ North direction (approx)

❶ To Junction 6 of M61
❷ A6027 Horwich link road
❸ South Stand (away)
❹ North Stand
❺ Nat Lofthouse Stand
❻ West Stand
❼ M61 northbound to M6 and Preston (at J6)
❽ M61 southbound to Manchester (at J6)
❾ To Horwich and Bolton
❿ To Lostock Junction BR station
⓫ To Horwich Parkway station

Above: 699055; Right: 699053

Ultimately a season which had promised much proved to be a disappointment. Perhaps it is a reflection of how far Wanderers have progressed in the Premier League that, having gone from perpetual strugglers, finishing in eighth position can now be regarded as a disappointment, given that in the previous year the club had finished sixth and thus brought European football to the Reebok for the first time. In 2006/07, Wanderers will be able to concentrate solely on domestic football, as eighth did not bring renewed entry into the UPFA Cup; moreover, the distractions caused by Sam Allardyce's name being featured in the list of possible England managers have also disappeared. The likelihood is that Wanderers will be more focused in 2006/07 and that a UEFA Cup spot should again be within the team's capabilities. As always, however, much will depend upon Allardyce's undoubted skills in bringing — and retaining — quality players to the Reebok.

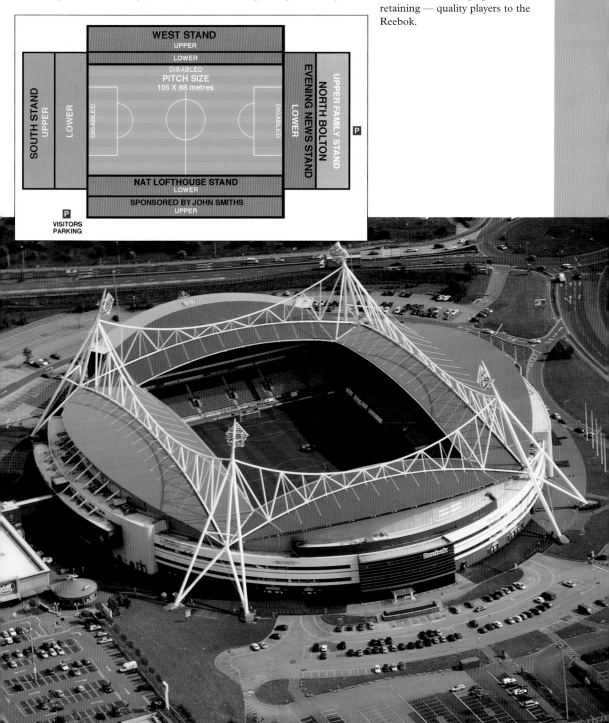

The Staffsmart Stadium, York Street, Boston, Lincolnshire PE21 6JN

Club Offices: 412-16 Redstone Industrial Estate, Boston, Lincolnshire PE21 8EA
Tel No: 0870 757 9266
Advance Tickets Tel No: 0870 757 9266
Fax: 01205 354063
Web Site: www.bufc.co.uk
E-mail: info@bufc.co.uk
League: League Two
Last Season: 11th (P46; W 15; D 16; L 15; GF 50; GA 60)
Nickname: The Pilgrims
Brief History: Boston Town was established in the 1880s and commenced playing at York Street. The club dropped the 'Town' suffix after World War 1 and re-formed as Boston United in 1934. The team won the Conference title in 1977 but was not allowed into the league due to the standard of the ground. The title was won again in 2002 and the club entered the Nationwide League at the start of the 2002/03 season. Record attendance 11,000
(Total) Current Capacity: 6,643 (1,769 seated)
Visiting Supporters' Allocation: 1,821 (no seated) in Town End Terrace

Club Colours: Amber and black hooped shirts, black shorts
Nearest Railway Station: Boston (one mile)
Parking (Car): Limited parking at the ground; recommended car park is the John Adams NCP
Parking (Coach/Bus): As directed
Police Force and Tel No: Lincolnshire (01205 366222)
Disabled Visitors Facilities:
  Wheelchairs: Finn Forest Stand
  Blind: No special facility
Future Development(s): The club has plans for the construction of a new 7,500-seat stadium in the Broadsides area of the town. The ground, anticipated to cost £8 million, will also provide a home for non-league Boston Town and is hoped to be available, subject to planning permission, by the start of the 2007/08 season. The work will be part funded by the sale of York Street and Tattershall Road (the home of Boston Town) for redevelopment.

KEY

E Entrance(s) for visiting supporters

R Refreshment bars for visiting supporters

T Toilets for visiting supporters

↑ North direction (approx)

❶ John Adams Way
❷ Spilsby Road
❸ Haven Bridge Road
❹ York Street
❺ Spayne Road
❻ River Witham
❼ Maud Foster Drain
❽ Market Place
❾ To bus and railway stations
❿ York Street Stand (away)
⓫ Spayne Road Terrace
⓬ Town End Terrace
⓭ Finnforest Stand

BOSTON UNITED

Above: 693105; *Right:* 693098

Having sold top scorer Andy Kirk to Northampton Town at the end of the 2004/05 season, it was always likely that the Pilgrims would struggle for goals and that proved to be the case for Steve Evans' team during 2005/06. However, the club did manage to improve its league position, finishing in 11th place only five points off the Play-Offs and, provided that such improvement is maintained into the 2006/07 season, then there is every possibility that the club could feature in the battle for the Play-Offs.

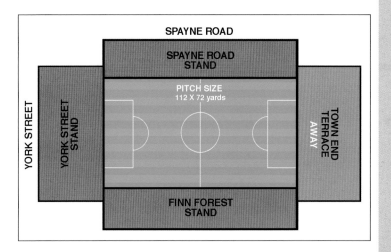

SPAYNE ROAD

SPAYNE ROAD
STAND

PITCH SIZE
112 X 72 yards

YORK STREET

YORK STREET
STAND

TOWN END
TERRACE
AWAY

FINN FOREST
STAND

The Fitness First Stadium at Dean Court, Bournemouth, Dorset, BH7 7AF

Tel No: 01202 726300
Advance Tickets Tel No: 0845 330 1000;
0120 726303
Fax: 01202 726301
E-Mail: enquiries@afcb.co.uk
Web Site: www.afcb.premiumtv.co.uk
League: League One
Last Season: 17th (P46; W 12; D 19; L 15; GF 48; GA 53)
Nickname: The Cherries
Brief History: Founded 1890 as Boscombe St. John's, changed to Boscombe (1899), Bournemouth & Boscombe Athletic (1923) and A.F.C. Bournemouth (1971). Former grounds Kings Park (twice) and Castlemain Road, Pokesdown. Moved to Dean Court in 1910. Record attendance 28,799; since rebuilding: 9,359

(Total) Current Capacity: 10,700 (all seated)
Visiting Supporters' Allocation: 1,500 in East Stand (can be increased to 2,000 if required)
Club Colours: Red and black shirts, black shorts
Nearest Railway Station: Bournemouth
Parking (Car): Large car park adjacent ground
Parking (Coach/Bus): Large car park adjacent ground
Police Force and Tel No: Dorset (01202 552099)
Disabled Visitors' Facilities:
  Wheelchairs: 100 spaces
  Blind: No special facility
Anticipated Development(s): The club still intends to construct a temporary South Stand at Dean Court, taking the ground's capacity to just under 11,000.

BOURNEMOUTH

KEY

C Club Offices

↑ North direction (approx)

❶ Car Park
❷ A338 Wessex Way
❸ To Bournemouth BR Station (1½ miles)
❹ To A31 & M27
❺ Thistlebarrow Road
❻ King's Park Drive
❼ Littledown Avenue
❽ North Stand
❾ Main Stand
❿ East Stand
⓫ Site of proposed South Stand

28

Above: 700388; Right: 700382

A difficult season at Dean Court for Sean O'Driscoll and the team saw the end of form from 2004/05 carry on into the new campaign with the result that the Cherries spent most of their time being more concerned about being dragged into the relegation zone rather than renewing efforts to reach the Play-Offs. Whilst never being sufficiently poor to be dragged into the relegation zone, the team hovered above the bottom four for most of the season and ultimately finished in 17th place some five points above relegated Hartlepool. Apart from indifferent form in the league, the Cherries were also one of the few teams to suffer embarrassment at the hands of non-league teams in the FA Cup when Tamworth defeated them 2-1 at Dean Court in the first round. Problems on the pitch were compounded by financial worries off it and it's hard to escape the conclusion that it's going to be another difficult season on the South Coast if Bournemouth are to escape the drop.

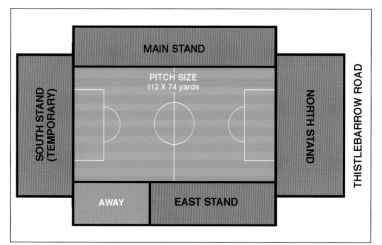

MAIN STAND

PITCH SIZE
112 X 74 yards

SOUTH STAND
(TEMPORARY)

NORTH STAND

THISTLEBARROW ROAD

AWAY

EAST STAND

Bradford & Bingley Stadium, Valley Parade, Bradford, BD8 7DY

Tel No: 0870 822 0000
Advance Tickets Tel No: 0870 822 1911
Fax: 01274 773356
Web Site: www.bradfordcityfc.premiumtv.co.uk
E-Mail: bradfordcityfc@compuserve.com
League: League One
Last Season: 11th (P 46; W 14; D 19; L 13; GF 51; GA 49)
Nickname: The Bantams
Brief History: Founded 1903 (formerly Manningham Northern Union Rugby Club founded in 1876). Continued use of Valley Parade, joined 2nd Division on re-formation. Record attendance: 39,146
(Total) Current Capacity: 25,136 (all seated)
Visiting Supporters' Allocation: 1,842 (all seated) in TL Dallas stand plus seats in Midland Road Stand if required
Club Colours: Claret and amber shirts, claret shorts

Nearest Railway Station: Bradford Forster Square
Parking (Car): Street parking and car parks
Parking (Coach/Bus): As directed by Police
Police Force and Tel No: West Yorkshire (01274 723422)
Disabled Visitors' Facilities:
   Wheelchairs: 110 places in Sunwin, CIBA and Carlsberg stands
   Blind: Commentary available
Anticipated Development(s): With work on the Main (Sunwin) Stand now completed, Valley Parade has a slightly imbalanced look. The club has proposals for the reconstruction of the Midland Road (Yorkshire First) Stand to take the ground's capacity to 30,000, although, given the club's current financial position, there is no time-scale.

KEY

C Club Offices
S Club Shop
E Entrance(s) for visiting supporters
R Refreshment bars for visiting supporters
T Toilets for visiting supporters

↑ North direction (approx)

❶ Midland Road
❷ Valley Parade
❸ A650 Manningham Lane
❹ To City Centre, Forster Square and Interchange BR Stations M606 & M62
❺ To Keighley
❻ Car Parks
❼ Sunwin Stand
❽ Midland (Yorkshire First) Stand
❾ TL Dallas Stand
❿ Carlsberg Stand

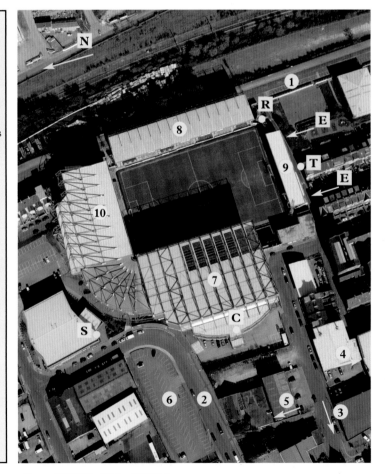

BRADFORD CITY

Above: 700121; *Right:* 700114

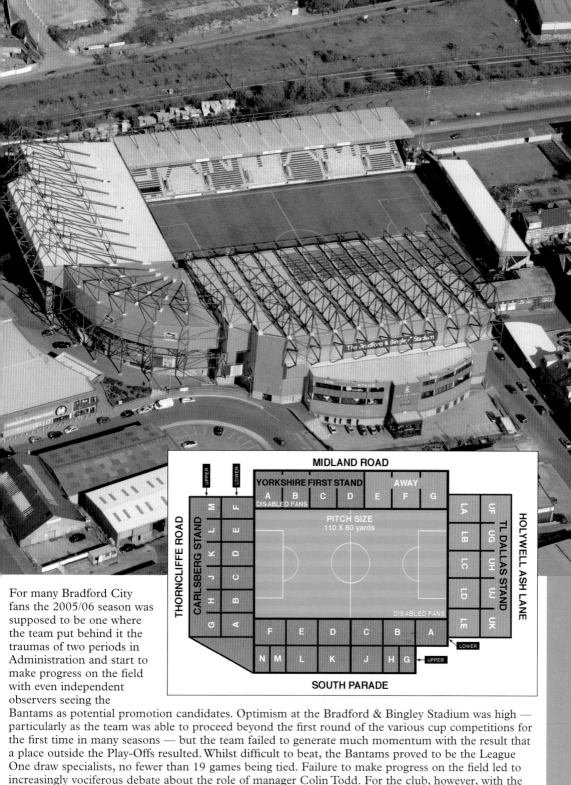

MIDLAND ROAD

YORKSHIRE FIRST STAND   AWAY

A   B   C   D   E   F   G

DISABLED FANS

PITCH SIZE
110 X 80 yards

UPPER LOWER

THORNCLIFFE ROAD

CARLSBERG STAND

M L K J H G

F E D C B A

DISABLED FANS

F E D C B A

N M L K J H G

LOWER

UPPER

LA LB LC LD LE

UF UG UH UJ UK

TL DALLAS STAND

HOLYWELL ASH LANE

SOUTH PARADE

For many Bradford City fans the 2005/06 season was supposed to be one where the team put behind it the traumas of two periods in Administration and start to make progress on the field with even independent observers seeing the Bantams as potential promotion candidates. Optimism at the Bradford & Bingley Stadium was high — particularly as the team was able to proceed beyond the first round of the various cup competitions for the first time in many seasons — but the team failed to generate much momentum with the result that a place outside the Play-Offs resulted. Whilst difficult to beat, the Bantams proved to be the League One draw specialists, no fewer than 19 games being tied. Failure to make progress on the field led to increasingly vociferous debate about the role of manager Colin Todd. For the club, however, with the talk of new investment, the new season could finally be one where the team starts to make a serious challenge to regain a place in the League Championship.

Griffin Park, Braemar Road, Brentford, Middlesex, TW8 0NT

Tel No: 0870 900 9229
Advance Tickets Tel No: 0870 900 9229
Fax: 020 8568 9940
Web Site: www.brentfordfc.premiumtv.co.uk
E-Mail: enquiries@brentfordfc.co.uk
League: League One
Last Season: 3rd (P46; W 20; D 16; L 10; GF 72; GA 52)
Nickname: The Bees
Brief History: Founded 1889. Former Grounds: Clifden House Ground, Benn's Field (Little Ealing), Shotters Field, Cross Roads, Boston Park Cricket Ground, moved to Griffin Park in 1904. Founder-members Third Division (1920). Record attendance 38,678
(Total) Current Capacity: 12,763 (8,905 seated)
Visiting Supporters' Allocation: 2,200 on Ealing Road Terrace (open) and 600 seats in Block A of Braemar Road Stand
Club Colours: Red and white striped shirts, black shorts
Nearest Railway Station: Brentford, South Ealing (tube)

Parking (Car): Street parking (restricted)
Parking (Coach/Bus): Layton Road car park
Other Club Sharing Ground: London Broncos RLFC
Police Force and Tel No: Metropolitan (020 8577 1212)
Disabled Visitors' Facilities:
  Wheelchairs: Braemar Road
  Blind: Commentary available
Anticipated Development(s): Although the club's long-term intention is to relocate, in mid-December 2004 it was announced that the Football Foundation would grant the club £1,775,950 for work at Griffin Park, provided that plans were approved at a public meeting. Planned work includes modification of the New Road Stand and the provision of a roof over the Ealing Road Terrace. Although the original application was rejected by the planning authorities in December, following local consultation plans were approved in mid-April. The work will ultimately result in a capacity of 15,000 at Griffin Park.

KEY

C Club Offices
S Club Shop
E Entrance(s) for visiting supporters

↑ North direction (approx)

❶ Ealing Road
❷ Braemar Road
❸ Brook Road South
❹ To M4 (¼ mile) & South Ealing Tube Station (1 mile)
❺ Brentford BR Station
❻ To A315 High Street & Kew Bridge
❼ New Road
❽ Ealing Road Terrace (away)
❾ Brook Road Stand

Above: 700195; *Right:* 700193

NEW ROAD

NEW STAND

PITCH SIZE
110 X 73 yards

BROOK ROAD

BROOK ROAD STAND

SEATS

COVERED TERRACE

DISABLED
FANS

EALING ROAD

EALING ROAD
TERRACE

UNCOVERED TERRACE
AWAY

PADDOCK

BRAEMAR ROAD STAND

AWAY

BRAEMAR ROAD

At times football can be a cruel sport and fans of the Bees must be thinking that at the end of a season that seemed to have promised much right until the end of the campaign. Apart from a not wholly unexpected victory over Premier League strugglers Sunderland in the fourth round of the FA Cup at Griffin Park, Brentford were in the hunt for automatic promotion right until the last day of the season. Unfortunately results on the last Saturday — Colchester's draw at Yeovil and Brentford's draw at Bournemouth — meant that the Essex team snatched the second automatic promotion spot and consigned the Bees to a Play-Off semi-final against sixth placed Swansea. A 1-1 draw in Swansea seemed to give Brentford the edge but two early goals by Leon Knight gave Swansea victory at Griffin Park and consigned Brentford to another season in League One. Away from the league, the first round of the Carling Cup saw the Bees defeated 5-0 away at Cheltenham and defeat Sunderland 2-1 in the fourth round of the FA Cup. At the end of the season Allen surprisingly announced his departure although the club initially refused to accept his resignation. As to the new season much will depend upon the squad that new manager Leroy Rosenior is able to keep and build; a number of important players are out of contract and, if the club is again to make a serious push for promotion, Rosenior will need to retain a number of them. The probability is that in 2006/07 the best that the club can hope for are perhaps the Play-Offs.

Withdean Stadium, Tongdean Lane, Brighton BN1 5JD

Tel No: 01273 695400
Fax: 01273 648179
Advance Ticket Tel No: 01273 776992
Web Site: www.seagulls.premiumtv.co.uk
E-Mail: seagulls@bhafc.co.uk
League: League Championship
Last Season: 24th (relegated) (P46; W 7; D 17; L 22; GF 39; GA 71)
Nickname: The Seagulls
Brief History: Founded 1900 as Brighton & Hove Rangers, changed to Brighton & Hove Albion 1902. Former grounds: Home Farm (Withdean), County Ground, Goldstone Ground (1902-1997), Priestfield Stadium (ground share with Gillingham) 1997-1999; moved to Withdean Stadium 1999. Founder members of the 3rd Division 1920. Record attendance (at Goldstone Ground): 36,747; at Withdean Stadium: 7,999.
(Total) Current Capacity: 8,850 (all seated)
Visiting Supporters' Allocation: 900 max on open West Stand
Club Colours: Blue and white striped shirts, white shorts
Nearest Railway Station: Preston Park
Parking (Cars): Street parking in the immediate vicinity of the ground is residents' only. This will be strictly enforced and it is suggested that intending visitors should use parking facilities away from the ground and use the proposed park and ride bus services that will be provided.
Parking (Coach/Bus): As directed
Police Force and Tel No: Sussex (01273 778922)
Disabled Visitors' Facilities
  Wheelchairs: Facilities in both North and South stands
  Blind: No special facility
Anticipated Development(s): After a four-year campaign, permission for the construction of the new ground at Falmer was given by John Prescott at the end of October 2005. It was planned that work on the 23,000-seat capacity ground will start during 2006 with the intention of completion for the start of the 2007/08 season. However, Lewes District Council launched a legal challenge to the construction of the new ground and, in early March, it was announced that this challenge would result in the ground being delayed with a new anticipated completion date of August 2009. A further development, on 6 April, resulted in the original approval being quashed as a result of a mistake made in John Prescott's original letter of approval with the result that the matter would again have to be referred to him.

KEY

Club Address:
8th Floor, Tower Point,
44 North Road, Brighton
BN1 1YR
Tel: 01273 695460
Fax: 01273 648179

Shop Address:
6 Queen's Road, Brighton

⬆ North direction (approx)

Note: All games at Withdean will be all-ticket with no cash admissions on the day.

❶ Withdean Stadium
❷ London-Brighton railway line
❸ To London Road (A23)
❹ Tongdean Lane
❺ Valley Drive
❻ To Brighton town centre and main railway station (1.75 miles)
❼ Tongdean Lane (with bridge under railway)
❽ South Stand
❾ A23 northwards to Crawley
❿ To Preston Park railway station
⓫ North Stand
⓬ North East Stand
⓭ West Stand (away)

Above: 699849; *Right:* 699861

A season of great disappointment both on and off the field saw the Seagulls' fight for a new stadium delayed following a legal challenge whilst the team also ultimately lost the battle to retain its League Championship status. Ironically, it was a home defeat against fellow strugglers Sheffield Wednesday that sent Brighton — as well as both Millwall and Crewe — down. The last time Brighton was relegated, the team made a swift return to the Championship; this time, with a number of well-resourced and ambitious teams already vying to escape to the Championship, it looks more difficult. Under Mark McGhee the team has the potential to do reasonably well in League One, but perhaps a Play-Off place is the best that can be expected.

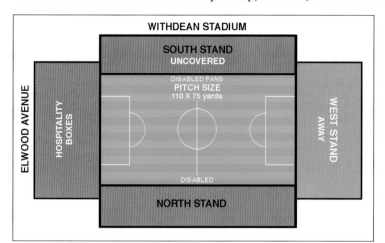

WITHDEAN STADIUM

SOUTH STAND
UNCOVERED

DISABLED FANS
PITCH SIZE
110 X 75 yards

DISABLED

ELWOOD AVENUE

HOSPITALITY BOXES

WEST STAND
AWAY

NORTH STAND

Ashton Gate Stadium, Ashton Road, Bristol BS3 2EJ

Tel No: 0117 963 0630
Advance Tickets Tel No: 0870 112 1897
Fax: 0117 963 0700
Web Site: www.bcfc.premiumtv.co.uk
E-Mail: sales@bcfc.co.uk
League: League One
Last Season: 9th (P 46; W 18; D 11; L 17; GF 66; GA 62
Nickname: The Robins
Brief History: Founded 1894 as Bristol South End changed to Bristol City in 1897. Former Ground: St John's Lane, Bedminster, moved to Ashton Gate in 1904. Record attendance 43,335
(Total) Current Capacity: 15,000 during redevelopment (all seated)
Visiting Supporters' Allocation: 3,000 in Wedlock End (all seated; can be increased to 5,500 if necessary) (location during redevelopment to be confirmed)
Club Colours: Red shirts, white shorts
Nearest Railway Station: Bristol Temple Meads

Parking (Car): Street parking
Parking (Coach/Bus): Marsh Road
Police Force and Tel No: Avon/Somerset (0117 927 7777)
Disabled Visitors' Facilities:
  Wheelchairs: Limited
  Blind: Commentary available
Anticipated Development(s): In February 2005 the club announced ambitious plans for the redevelopment of Ashton Gate with the intention of creating a 30,000 all-seated stadium. The first phase of the work, the replacement of the East (Wedlock) Stand with a new £7 million structure, was due to have started in 2005. However, delays mean work is now likely to take place during the 2006/07 season. Whilst the work is in progress, the ground's capacity will be reduced to 15,000 and on completion, the overall capacity will be increased to 21,000. Once work on the East Stand is completed, the club's attentions will turn to the Williams and Donman stands.

BRISTOL CITY

KEY
C Club Offices
S Club Shop

↑ North direction (approx)

❶ A370 Ashton Road
❷ A3209 Winterstoke Road
❸ To Temple Meads Station (1½ miles
❹ To City Centre, A4, M32 & M4
❺ Database Wedlock Stand (prior to redevelopment)
❻ Atyeo Stand
❼ Brunel Ford Williams Stand
❽ Dolman Stand

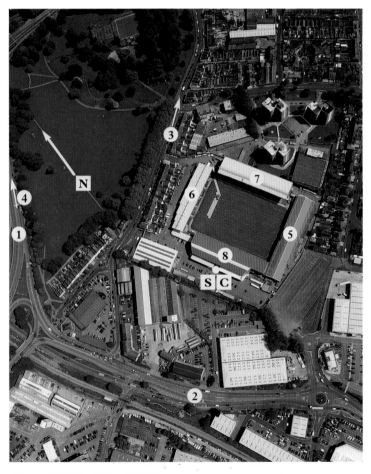

Above: 699164; *Right:* 699177

Although one of the pre-season favourites, an abysmal start to the campaign culminating in a 7-1 defeat away at newly promoted Swansea City that left the team in the relegation zone (shortly after a 4-2 home defeat by Barnet in the Carling Cup), saw Brian Tinnion depart from Ashton Gate after just over a year in charge in mid-September. Keith Millen, the Assistant Manager, took over as caretaker in the brief period before ex-Yeovil boss Gary Johnson took over the reins. As is often the case, the arrival of a new regime brought an immediate result in the shape of a 3-2 victory away at high-flying Brentford and that was to set the tone for much of the season, except for a slight hiccup, with City ultimately mounting a late, but unfulfilled, challenge for the Play-Offs — indeed, if the results had gone in City's favour on the last day City could have sneaked into them (in fact the Robins would have needed Swansea to lose and beat Southend at Roots Hall by a double-figure score — neither of which happened!). However, the late season form will have encouraged the Ashton Gate faithful in the belief that 2006/07 will indeed be the team's chance for promotion and certainly the Play-Offs should be within the club's abilities.

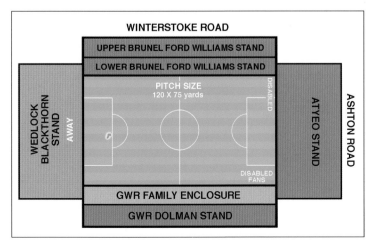

The Memorial Stadium, Filton Avenue, Horfield, Bristol BS7 0BF

Tel No: 0117 909 6648
Advance Tickets Tel No: 0117 909 6648
Fax: 0117 907 4312
Web Site: www.bristolrovers.premiumtv.co.uk
E-Mail: club@bristolrovers.co.uk
League: League Two
Last Season: 12th (P46; W 17; D 9; L 20; GF 59; GA 67)
Nickname: The Pirates (or Gasheads historically)
Brief History: Founded 1883 as Black Arabs, changed to Eastville Rovers (1884), Bristol Eastville Rovers (1896) and Bristol Rovers (1897). Former grounds: Purdown, Three Acres, The Downs (Horfield), Ridgeway, Bristol Stadium (Eastville), Twerton Park (1986-96), moved to The Memorial Ground 1996. Record attendance: (Eastville) 38,472, (Twerton Park) 9,813, (Memorial Ground) 11,433
(Total) Current Capacity: 11,917 (4,000 seated); standing capacity of 8,000 includes 500 on the Family Terrace
Visiting Supporters' Allocation: 1,132 (Centenary Stand Terrace; open)
Club Colours: Blue and white quartered shirts, white shorts

Nearest Railway Station: Filton or Stapleton Road
Parking (Car): Limited parking at ground for home fans only; street parking also available
Parking (Coach/Bus): As directed
Police Force and Tel No: Avon/Somerset (0117 927 7777)
Other Clubs Sharing Ground: Bristol Shoguns RUFC
Disabled Visitors' Facilities:
  Wheelchairs: 35 wheelchair positions
  Blind: Limited provision
Anticipated Development(s): Although the club had sought and been granted planning permission in 2005 for the redevelopment of the Blackthorn End to create a 13,000-seat ground, the club's plans are now more ambitious and involve the complete redevelopment of the ground, with four new stands proving 19,000 sears. The work will also include the slight relocation to the east of the pitch. There is, however, no timescale for this work at present.stands proving 19,000 sears. The club has also announced that it may temporaly relocate in order to expedite this work.

BRISTOL ROVERS

KEY

C Rugby Club offices
E Entrance(s) for visiting supporters
R Refrshments for visiting supporters
T Toilets for visiting supporters

↑ North direction (approx)

❶ Filton Avenue
❷ Gloucester Road
❸ To Muller Road
❹ To Bristol city centre (2.5 miles) and BR Temple Meads station (3 miles)
❺ Downer Road
❻ Car Park
❼ To M32 J2 (1.5 miles)
❽ Strathmore Road
❾ To Filton (1.5 miles)
❿ Hill House Hammond Stand
⓫ West (Das) Stand
⓬ Blackthorn End
⓭ South Stand

Above: 700378; *Right:* 700373

Following City's lead, the Pirates sacked Ian Atkins as manager in late September after an 18-month reign following a 4-0 drubbing at Chester which meant that the team had secured nine points from nine games and stood at 19th position in League Two. Player-coach Paul Trollope was immediately appointed as caretaker and was later confirmed in the post. Under Trollope's control the club gradually pulled away from the drop zone, ultimately finishing in 12th place, closer to the Play-Offs than the drop zone. Provided that Trollope retains the key members of his squad, and there are rumours about the loss of several influential players at the time of writing, then 2005/06 has lain the foundations for a more sustained challenge on the Play-Offs.

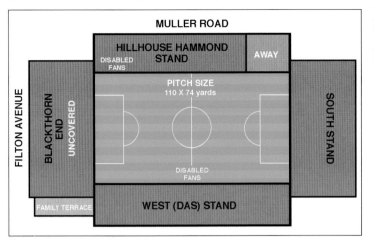

MULLER ROAD

HILLHOUSE HAMMOND STAND

DISABLED FANS

AWAY

FILTON AVENUE

BLACKTHORN END

UNCOVERED

PITCH SIZE
110 X 74 yards

SOUTH STAND

DISABLED FANS

FAMILY TERRACE

WEST (DAS) STAND

Turf Moor, Harry Potts Way, Burnley, Lancs, BB10 4BX

Tel No: 0870 443 1882
Advance Tickets Tel No: 0870 443 1914
Fax: 01282 700014
Web Site: www.burnleyfootballclub.premium.co.uk
E-Mail: info@burnleyfc.com
League: League Championship
Last Season: 17th (P46; W 14; D 12; L 20; GF 46; GA 54)
Nickname: The Clarets
Brief History: Founded 1882, Burnley Rovers (Rugby Club) combined with another Rugby Club, changed to soccer and name to Burnley. Moved from Calder Vale to Turf Moor in 1882. Founder-members Football League (1888). Record attendance 54,775
(Total) Current Capacity: 22,546 (all seated)
Visiting Supporters' Allocation: 4,125 (all seated in David Fishwick [Cricket Field] Stand)
Club Colours: Claret and blue shirts, white shorts

Nearest Railway Station: Burnley Central
Parking (Car): Church Street and Fulledge Rec. (car parks)
Parking (Coach/Bus): As directed by Police
Police Force and Tel No: Lancashire (01282 425001)
Disabled Visitors' Facilities:
  Wheelchairs: Places available in North, East and Cricket Field stands
  Blind: Headsets provided with commentary
Anticipated Development(s): The club has proposals for the redevelopment of the Cricket Field (David Fishwick) Stand but this depends on the relocation of the cricket club. The new structure would provide seating for some 7,000. In the event of this option not proving practical attention will turn to the expansion of the Bob Lord Stand.

KEY

C Club Offices
S Club Shop
E Entrance(s) for visiting supporters

↑ North direction (approx)

❶ Brunshaw Road
❷ Belvedere Road
❸ Burnley Central BR Station (½ mile)
❹ Cricket Ground
❺ Cricket Field Stand
❻ East (Jimmy McIlroy) Stand
❼ Bob Lord Stand
❽ North (James Hargreaves) Stand

Above: 700153; *Right:* 700160

JAMES HARGREAVES (LONGSIDE)
UPPER
LOWER

PITCH SIZE
112 X 70 yards

DISABLED FANS

DISABLED FANS

BOB LORD STAND

BRUNSHAW ROAD

BELVEDERE ROAD

CRICKET FIELD
(DAVID FISHWICK)
STAND

AWAY

JIMMY McILROY
STAND

UPPER

LOWER

DISABLED FANS

BEE HOLE LANE

In Steve Cotterill's second season in charge at Turf Moor, the Clarets had a relatively disappointing season with, at one stage, it appearing that the club would get sucked in to the relegation battle. In the event, however, the club was to finish in 17th place — poor in comparison to the position achieved the previous year but still some 12 points above relegated Crewe — and, with the promoted teams coming up from League One looking relatively weak, the team should be capable of improving upon this in 2006/07. The one concern, however, is the team's lack of prowess up front; an average of a goal a game, whilst not the worst in the division, was worse than relegated Crewe's total and, if it hadn't been for a relatively mean defence, the Clarets' plight might have been even worse.

Gigg Lane, Bury, Lancashire, BL9 9HR

Tel No: 0161 764 4881
Advance Tickets Tel No: 0161 705 21441
Fax: 0161 764 5521
Web Site: www.buryfc.co.uk
E-Mail: info@buryfc.co.uk
League: League Two
Last Season: 19th (P 46; W 12; D 17; L 17; GF 45; GA 57)
Nickname: The Shakers
Brief History: Founded 1885, no former names or former grounds. Record attendance 35,000
(Total) Current Capacity: 11,669 (all seated)
Visiting Supporters' Allocation: 2,676 (all seated) in West (Manchester Road) Stand
Club Colours: White shirts, royal blue shorts

Nearest Railway Station: Bury Interchange
Parking (Car): Street parking
Parking (Coach/Bus): As directed by Police
Police Force and Tel No: Greater Manchester (0161 872 5050)
Other clubcs sharing ground: FC United of Manchester
Disabled Visitors' Facilities:
  Wheelchairs: South Stand (home) and West Stand (away)
  Blind: Commentary available
Anticipated Development(s): The completion of the rebuilt Cemetery End means that current plans for the redevelopment of Gigg Lane have been completed.

KEY

C Club Offices
S Club Shop
E Entrance(s) for visiting supporters

⬆ North direction (approx)

❶ Car Park
❷ Gigg Lane
❸ To A56 Manchester Road
❹ To Town Centre & Bury Interchange (Metrolink) (¾ mile)
❺ West (Manchester Road) Stand
❻ Cemetery End

Above: 700091; *Right:* 700097

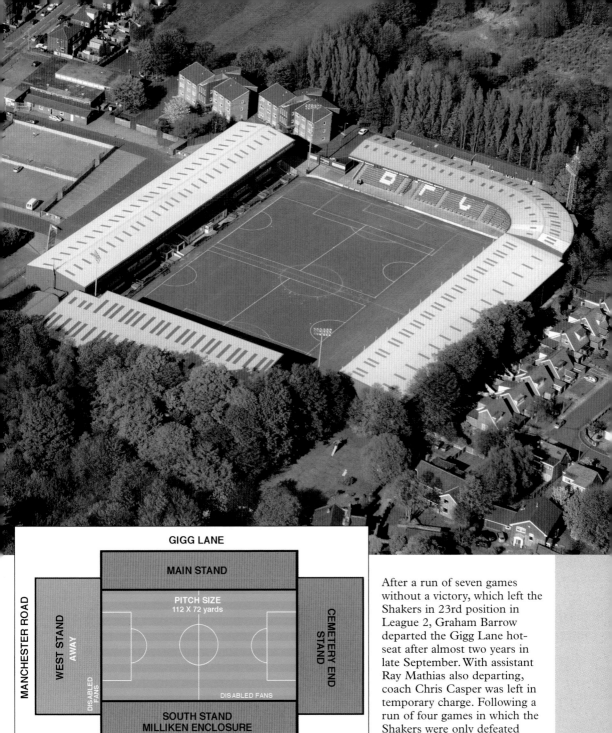

GIGG LANE

MAIN STAND

MANCHESTER ROAD

WEST STAND
AWAY

DISABLED FANS

PITCH SIZE
112 X 72 yards

DISABLED FANS

CEMETERY END STAND

SOUTH STAND
MILLIKEN ENCLOSURE

After a run of seven games without a victory, which left the Shakers in 23rd position in League 2, Graham Barrow departed the Gigg Lane hot-seat after almost two years in late September. With assistant Ray Mathias also departing, coach Chris Casper was left in temporary charge. Following a run of four games in which the Shakers were only defeated once, Casper was confirmed as new manager in mid-October.

At 30, he became one of the youngest managers in the history of the Football League. Under Caspar's management Bury managed to retain its Football League status — but only just. If results on the last day had gone against them, the Shakers could well have been facing the Conference rather than renewing acquaintances with Accrington Stanley after a gap of some 44 years. A last day 2-2 draw at equally threatened Notts County was sufficient to see Bury survive for another season, but it looks as though it will be another hard season both on and off the field if Bury are to survive the drop again.

Ninian Park, Sloper Road, Cardiff, CF11 8SX

Tel No: 029 2022 1001
Advance Tickets Tel No: 0845 345 1400
Fax: 029 2034 1148
Web Site: www.cardiffcityfc.premiumtv.co.uk
E-mail: club@cardiffcityfc.co.uk
League: League Championship
Last Season: 11th (P46; W 16; D 12; L 18; GF 58; GA 59)
Nickname: The Bluebirds
Brief History: Founded 1899. Former Grounds: Riverside Cricket Club, Roath, Sophia Gardens, Cardiff Arms Park and The Harlequins Rugby Ground, moved to Ninian Park in 1910. Ground record attendance 61,566 (Wales v. England, 1961)
(Total) Current Capacity: 20,000 (12,647 seated)
Visiting Supporters' Allocation: 2,000 maximum in John Smiths Grange End Terrace (limited seating)
Club Colours: Blue shirts, blue shorts

Nearest Railway Station: Ninian Park (adjacent) (Cardiff Central 1 mile)
Parking (Car): Opposite Ground, no street parking around ground
Parking (Coach/Bus): Leckith Stadium car park
Police Force and Tel No: South Wales (029 2022 2111)
Disabled Visitors' Facilities:
Wheelchairs: Corner Canton Stand/Popular Bank (covered)
Blind: No special facility
Anticipated Development(s): The club is still progressing with its plans for a new 30,000-seat stadium at Leckith, close to Ninian Park, where the existing athletics stadium would be replaced. The £100 million scheme is likely to include other commercial activities but there is at present no confirmed time-scale for the work.

KEY

C Club Offices
S Club Shop
E Entrance(s) for visiting supporters
R Refreshment bars for visiting supporters
T Toilets for visiting supporters (Terrace only, when used)

↑ North direction (approx)

❶ Sloper Road
❷ B4267 Leckwith Road
❸ Car Park
❹ To A4232 & M4 Junction 33 (8 miles)
❺ Ninian Park Road
❻ To City Centre & Cardiff Central BR Station (1 mile)
❼ To A48 Western Avenue, A49M, and M4 Junction 32 and 29
❽ Ninian Park BR station

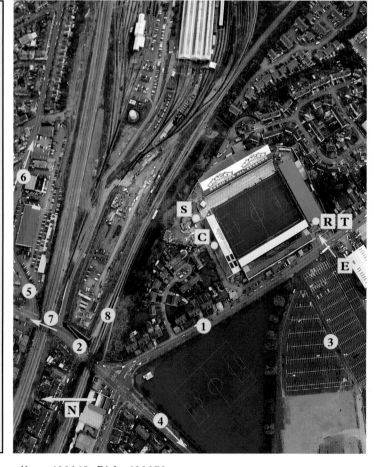

Above: 699068; *Right:* 699079

Under new manager Dave Jones, appointed in the summer of 2005, the Bluebirds had a more successful campaign in 2005/06 than in the previous year when relegation haunted the corridors of Ninian Park. Whilst never threatening to make a sustained challenge for the Play-Off places, the Bluebirds improved their standing in the League Championship, gaining five places over that achieved in 2004/05 in finishing in 11th place. Provided that Jones can improve the squad during the close season — in particular bring a proven striker to a club that struggled to score goals during the season — then there may be further progress. However, It's hard to escape the conclusion that in a highly competitive Championship, City will be one of those teams too good to go down but not good enough to take on the ex-Premier League teams for promotion or even the Play-Offs.

NINIAN PARK ROAD

POPULAR BANK STAND

OPPEN PADDOCK

DISABLED FANS

PITCH SIZE
110 X 70 yards

SPAR FAMILY (CANTON) STAND

JOHN SMITHS GRANGE END

AWAY

F | E | D | C | B | A

GRANDSTAND

SLOPER ROAD

Brunton Park, Warwick Road, Carlisle, CA1 1LL

Telephone: 01228 526237
Advance Tickets Tel No: 01228 526327
Fax: 01228 554141
Web Site: www.carlisleunited.premiumtv.co.uk
E-mail: enquiries@carlisleunited.co.uk
League: League One
Last Season: 1st (promoted) (P 46; W 25; D 11; L 10; GF 84; GA 42)
Nickname: The Cumbrians or the Blues
Brief History: Founded 1904 as Carlisle United (previously named Shaddongate United). Former Grounds: Millholme Bank and Devonshire Park, moved to Brunton Park in 1909. Record attendance 27,500
(Total) Current Capacity: 12,291 (6,433 seated)

Visiting Supporters' Allocation: 1,700 (Petterill End Terrace — open — or north end of Main Stand)
Club Colours: Blue shirts, white shorts
Nearest Railway Station: Carlisle
Parking (Car): Rear of ground
Parking (Coach/Bus): St Aiden's Road car park
Police Force and Tel No: Cumbria (01228 528191)
Disabled Visitors' Facilities:
Wheelchairs: East Stand and Paddock (prior arrangement)
Blind: No special facilities
Anticipated Development(s):

CARLISLE UNITED

KEY

C Club Offices
E Entrance(s) for visiting supporters
R Refreshment bars for visiting supporters
T Toilets for visiting supporters

↑ North direction (approx)

❶ A69 Warwick Road
❷ To M6 Junction 43
❸ Carlisle Citadel BR station (1 mile)
❹ Greystone Road
❺ Car Park
❻ Petterill End (away)
❼ Cumberland Bulding Society (East) Stand

Above: 699882; *Right:* 699091

A triumphant return to the Football League saw Carlisle United as one of the dominant teams in League Two during the season and it came as no surprise that Paul Simpson's team achieved both automatic promotion and the divisional championship. The team's success was ensured both by the most potent strike force in the division — a total of 84 goals scored — with one of the meanest defences — only 42 goals conceded in the league. As both Southend and Swansea proved in 2005/06, teams that come up from League Two can thrive at this higher level and there is every possibility that Carlisle can do as well. Whilst automatic promotion may be beyond the team, there is every likelihood that the squad can make the Play-Offs. After the end of the season Simpson departed to take over Preston. He was replaced by Neil McDonald.

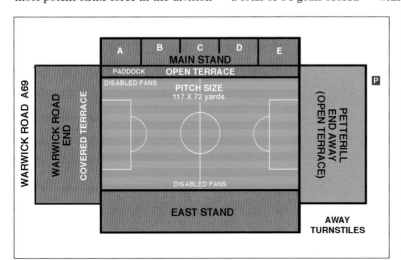

The Valley, Floyd Road, Charlton, London, SE7 8BL

Tel No: 020 8333 4000
Advance Tickets Tel No: 020 8333 4010
Fax: 020 8333 4001
Web Site: www.cafc.co.uk
E-Mail: info@cafc.co.uk
League: F.A. Premier
Last Season: 13th (P 38; W 13; D 8; L 17; GF 41; GA 55)
Nickname: The Addicks
Brief History: Founded 1905. Former grounds: Siemens Meadows, Woolwich Common, Pound Park, Angerstein Athletic Ground, The Mount Catford, Selhurst Park (Crystal Palace FC), Boleyn Ground (West Ham United FC), The Valley (1912-23, 1924-85, 1992-date). Founder Members 3rd Division South. Record attendance 75,031
(Total) Current Capacity: 27,116 (all seated)
Visiting Supporters' Allocation: 3,000 (maximum; all seated in South Stand)

Club Colours: Red shirts, white shorts
Nearest Railway Station: Charlton
Parking (Car): Street parking
Parking (Coach/Bus): As directed by Police
Police Force and Tel No: Metropolitan (020 8853 8212)
Disabled Visitors' Facilities:
  Wheelchairs: East/West/South stands
  Blind: Commentary, 12 spaces
Anticipated Development(s): The club presented plans to Greenwich Council in mid-December for the redevelopment of the East Stand, taking the ground's capacity to 31,000. At the same time the club lodged outline plans for the redevelopment of the rest of the stadium with the intention of taking capacity to 40,600.

CHARLTON ATHLETIC

KEY

E Entrance(s) for visiting supporters

R Refreshment bars for visiting supporters

T Toilets for visiting supporters

↑ North Direction (approx)

❶ Harvey Gardens
❷ A206 Woolwich Road
❸ Valley Grove
❹ Floyd Road
❺ Charlton BR Station
❻ East Stand
❼ North Stand
❽ West stand
❾ South stand (away)
❿ Charlton Church Lane
⓫ Charlton Lane

Above: 699307; *Right:* 699295

A season that seemed to have promised much at The Valley, with Charlton amongst the early Premier League pacesetters, ultimately turned into another campaign of mid-table mediocrity and, with the resignation of Alan Curbishley at the end of the season, an undoubted feeling that the end of an era had been reached. Curbishley had held the managerial role at The Valley for some 15 years — making him the second longest surviving manager in the Premier League — and had ensured during his tenure that Charlton had become one of the established Premier League teams. In late May the club announced that ex-Crystal Palace boss Iain Dowie had agreed to take over at the Valley. Dowie inherits a team that seems incapable of mounting a season-long campaign; if he can get his squad to perform for all 38 league games then there is every possibility that the team could make a challenge for a UEFA Cup spot. If, however, previous years' form is replicated another season of mid-table mediocrity beckons.

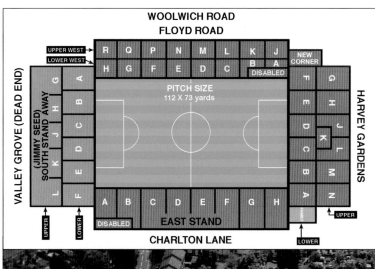

Stamford Bridge, Fulham Road, London, SW6 1HS

Tel No: 0870 300 23221
Advance Tickets Tel No: 0870 300 2322
Fax: 020 7381 4831
E-Mail: No contact available for general inquiries via e-mail
Web Site: www.chelseafc.com
League: F.A. Premier
Last Season: 1st (P 38; W 29; D 4; L 5; GF 72; GA 22)
Nickname: The Blues
Brief History: Founded 1905. Admitted to Football League (2nd Division) on formation. Stamford Bridge venue for F.A. Cup Finals 1919-22. Record attendance 82,905
(Total) Current Capacity: 42,449 (all seated)
Visiting Supporters' Allocation: Approx. 1,600 (East Stand Lower; can be increased to 3,200 if required or 5,200 if part of the Matthew Harding Stand [lower tier] is allocated)

Club Colours: Blue shirts, blue shorts
Nearest Railway Station: Fulham Broadway or West Brompton
Parking (Car): Street parking and underground car park at ground
Parking (Coach/Bus): As directed by Police
Police Force and Tel No: Metropolitan (020 7385 1212)
Disabled Visitors' Facilities:
  Wheelchairs: East Stand
  Blind: No special facility
Anticipated Development(s): With the long awaited completion of the second tier of the West Stand now achieved, redevelopment of Stamford Bridge as a stadium is now complete.

KEY

⬆ North direction (approx)

❶ A308 Fulham Road
❷ Central London
❸ To Fulham Broadway Tube Station
❹ Mathew Harding Stand
❺ East Stand
❻ West Stand
❼ South (Shed) Stand
❽ West Brompton Station

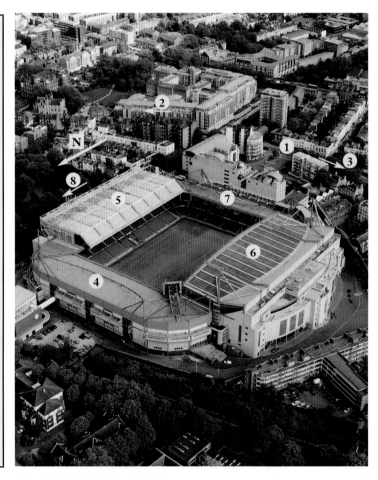

Above: 700208; *Right:* 700211

CHELSEA

As widely expected, José Mourinho's side retained the Premier League title although it was not as clear cut as the first title in 2004/05 and the abiding memory of the campaign was not the winning of the title itself but Mourinho's churlishness during the season. Whilst it is undoubtedly true that Chelsea did produce some excellent football during the year — and it's particularly good to see three English players at the heart of the Chelsea squad unlike many other top Premier League teams — it's also true that that there's an undercurrent of gamesmanship and an attitude of the 'whole world's against us', which is a curse of every successful team. Away from the League, Chelsea made the knock-out stages of the Champions League but were defeated 3-2 by eventual winners Barcelona and, in the FA Cup, reached the Semi-Finals only to be defeated this time by Liverpool. With Mourinho again strengthening his squad during the close season — with Michael Ballack already confirmed as joining the champions for the new campaign — the Blues look well equipped again to make it a fairly safe bet that the Premier League title will again be heading to West London — despite improved squads amongst the main contenders — but until Chelsea reach — and win — a Champions League final, the club won't be able to claim to have truly reached the heights.

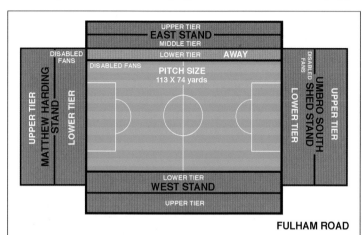

Whaddon Road, Cheltenham, Gloucestershire GL52 5NA

Tel No: 01242 573558
Advance Tickets Tel No: 01242 573558
Fax: 01242 224675
Web Site: www.cheltenhamtownfc.premiumtv.co.uk
E-Mail: info@ctfc.com
League: League One
Last Season: 5th (promoted) (P 46; W 19; D 15; L 14; GF 65; GA 53)
Nickname: The Robins
Brief History: Cheltenham Town was founded in 1892. It moved to Whaddon Road in 1932 having previously played at Carter's Field. After two seasons in the Conference it achieved Nationwide League status at the end of the 1998/99 season. Record attendance 8,326
(Total) Current Capacity: 7,066 (3,912 seated)
Visiting Supporters' Allocation: 2,600 (maximum) in Whaddon Road Terrace – uncovered – and in Wymans Road (In2Print) Stand

Club Colours: Red and white striped shirts, white shorts
Nearest Railway Station: Cheltenham (1.5 miles)
Parking (Car): Limited parking at ground; otherwise on-street
Parking (Coach/Bus): As directed by Police
Police Force and Tel No: Gloucestershire (01242 521321)
Disabled Visitors' Facilities:
  Wheelchairs: Six spaces in front of Main Stand
  Blind: No special facility
Anticipated Development(s): Work on the open Whaddon Road Terrace commenced after last year's edition went to print and the new structure — called the Carlsberg Stand — was opened in December 2005. This structure provides accommodation for 1,100 fans. The next phase in the development of Whaddon Road will involve the rebuilding of the Main Stan but there is at present no timescale for this work.

CHELTENHAM TOWN

KEY
C Club Offices
E Entrance(s) for visiting supporters

↑ North direction (approx)

❶ B4632 Prestbury Road
❷ Cromwell Road
❸ Whaddon Road
❹ Wymans Road
❺ To B4075 Priors Road
❻ To B4075 Prior Road
❼ To Cheltenham town centre and railway station (1.5 and 2 miles respectively)
❽ Main Stand
❾ Wymans Road Stand
❿ Prestbury Road End
⓫ Carlsberg Stand (away)

Above: 699755; Right: 699762

A season of some success at Whaddon Road sees John Ward's team exchange derbies with Bristol Rovers for ones with Bristol City as the club makes the leap from League Two to League One. Whilst never making a serious challenge for one of the automatic promotion places, the Robins were assured of a Play-Off place and faced Wycombe Wanderers over two legs in the Semi-Finals. Victory meant a trip to the Millennium Stadium where Grimsby Town lay in wait. Grimsby had just missed out on promotion in the last minute of the normal season and, in finishing six points ahead of Cheltenham, must have fancied their chances. In the event, however, a 1-0 victory was sufficient to bring League One football back to Whaddon Road. However, as a team promoted through the Play-Offs, the Robins will be widely considered as favourites for an immediate return to League Two and it's probable that the team will struggle to retain its League One status. At best, perhaps, a season of consolidation but also the chance to renew acquaintance with Brentford, who the Robins defeated 5-0 in the first round of the Carling cup in 2005/06.

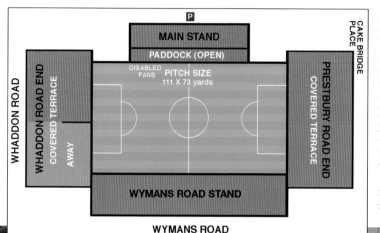

Saunders Honda Stadium, Bumpers Lane, Chester, CH1 4LT

Tel No: 01244 371376
Advance Tickets Tel No: 01244 371376
Fax: 01244 390265
Web-site: www.chestercityfc.net
E-mail: info@chestercityfc.net
League: League Two
Last Season: 15th (P 46; W 14; D 12; L 20; GF 53; GA 59)
Nickname: The Blues
Brief History: Founded 1884 from amalgamation of Chester Wanderers and Chester Rovers. Former Grounds: Faulkner Street, Lightfoot Street, Whipcord Lane, Sealand Road Moss Lane (Macclesfield Town FC), moved to Deva Stadium 1992. Record attendance (Sealand Road) 20,500; (Deva Stadium) 5,987

(Total) Current Capacity: 6,012 (3,284) seated
Visiting Supporters' Allocation: 1,896 maximum (seated 600 maximum) in South Terrace and West Stand
Club Colours: Blue/White striped shirts, Blue shorts
Nearest Railway Station: Chester (three miles)
Parking (Car): Car park at ground
Parking(Coach/Bus): Car park at ground
Police Force and Tel No: Cheshire (01244 350222)
Disabled Visitors' Facilities:
  Wheelchairs: West and East Stand
  Blind: Facility available
Anticipated Development(s):

CHESTER CITY

KEY

C Club Offices
S Club Shop
E Entrance(s) for visiting supporters
R Refreshment bars for visiting supporters
T Toilets for visiting supporters

⬆ North direction (approx)

❶ Bumpers Lane
❷ To City centre and Chester railway station (1.5 miles)
❸ Car park
❹ South Terrace
❺ West Stand

Above: 697211; *Right:* 697204

With the club in a run of 11 defeats in 12 games following a 2-0 reverse at Leyton Orient which left the team only four points above the League Two drop zone having been threatening for a Play-Off spot earlier in the campaign, Keith Curle departed as City manager at the end of February after a nine-month stint in the Deva Stadium hot-seat. The club moved quickly in appointing ex-boss Mark Wright, who had left 18 months earlier, as manager until the end of the season. Under Wright the club's position was stabilised and the team gradually pulled away from the drop zone. Ultimately, the team finished in 15th position, five points above relegated Oxford but 12 below the Play-Offs. With Wright confirmed as manager for the 2006/07 season, there will be expectations at the Deva Stadium that the club can progress and improve on the 2005/06 season. Realistically, however, it looks as though City will again feature amongst the also-rans, with a position of mid-table mediocrity beckoning.

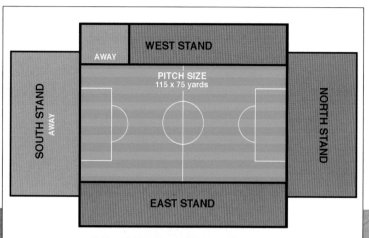

WEST STAND

AWAY

PITCH SIZE
115 x 75 yards

SOUTH STAND

AWAY

NORTH STAND

EAST STAND

Recreation Ground, Saltergate, Chesterfield, S40 4SX

Tel No: 01246 209765
Advance Tickets Tel No: 01246 209765
Fax: 01246 556799
Web Site: www.chesterfield-fc.premiumtv.co.uk
E-Mail: suegreen@therecreationground.co.uk
League: League One
Last Season: 16th (P 46; W 14; D 14; L 18; GF 63; GA 73)
Nickname: The Spireites
Brief History: Found 1886. Former Ground: Spital Vale. Formerly named Chesterfield Town. Record attendance 30,968
(Total) Current Capacity: 8,504 (2,674 seated)
Visiting Supporters' Allocation: 1,850 maximum (maximum 450 seated)
Club Colours: Blue and white shirts, white shorts
Nearest Railway Station: Chesterfield

Parking (Car): Saltergate car park, street parking
Parking (Coach/Bus): As directed by Police
Police Force and Tel No: Derbyshire (01246 220100)
Disabled Visitors' Facilities:
  Wheelchairs: Saltergate Stand
  Blind: No special facility
Anticipated Development(s): The club's supporters voted in favour of relocation in the summer of 2003 and the club is now actively pursuing relocation to the site of the former Dema glassworks about one mile from the town centre with Alfred McAlpine as the proposed contractor. Assuming that the necessary planning permission is granted, the 11,000-seat ground should be completed for the start of the 2008/09 season.

KEY

C Club Offices
S Club Shop
E Entrance(s) for visiting supporters
R Refreshment bars for visiting supporters
T Toilets for visiting supporters

⬆ North direction (approx)

❶ Saltergate
❷ Cross Street
❸ St Margaret's Drive
❹ West Bars
❺ To A617 & M1 Junction 29
❻ To station and town centre
❼ Compton Street Terrace
❽ Cross Street End (away)

Above: 699864; Right: 699877

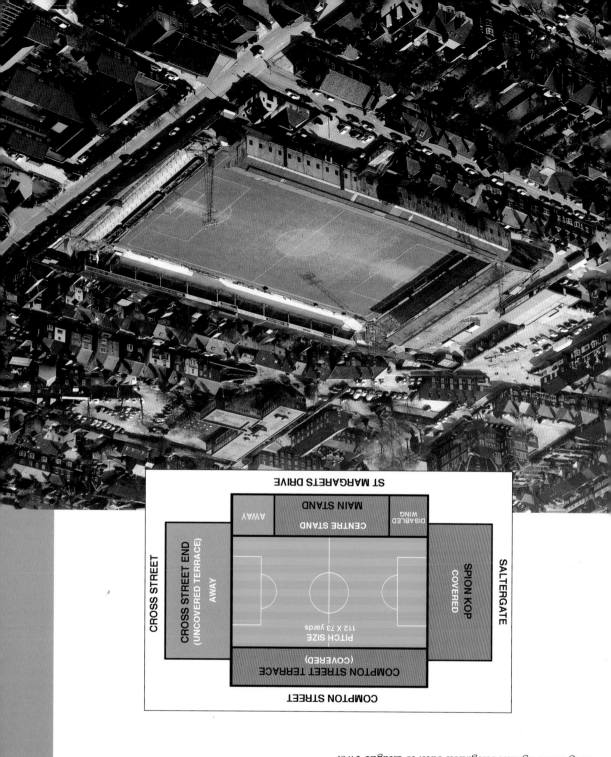

Under Roy McFarland, the Spireites seemed, for part of the season, to be making a serious effort towards a top-half finish; in the event, however, the club was to finish in 16th place — still its best league position for almost a decade — and a slight improvement over that achieved at the end of 2004/05. However, such was the tightness of League One in 2005/06 that the team only finished six points above the drop zone and a poor start to the new campaign could again see the team facing a long battle against relegation back to League Two.

Layer Road Ground, Colchester, CO2 7JJ

Tel No: 0871 226 2161

Advance Tickets Tel No: 087 226 2161

Fax: 01206 715327

Web Site: www.cu-fc.premiumtv.co.uk

E-Mail: caroline@colchesterunited.net

League: League Championship

Last Season: 2nd (promoted) (P 46; W 22; D 13; L 11; GF 58; GA 40)

Nickname: The U's

Brief History: Founded 1937, joined Football League 1950, relegated 1990, promoted 1992. Record attendance 19,072

(Total) Current Capacity: 6,200 (1,877 seated)

Visiting Supporters' Allocation: 650 in Layer Road End (standing) plus 200 seats (East Coast Cable Stand)

Club Colours: Royal blue and white shirts, blue shorts

Nearest Railway Station: Colchester Town

Parking (Car): Street parking

Parking (Coach/Bus): Boadicea Way

Police Force and Tel No: Essex (01206 762212)

Disabled Visitors' Facilities:

Wheelchairs: Space for 12 in front of terrace (next to Main Stand)

Blind: Space for 3 blind persons and 3 guides (two regularly occupied by home supporters)

Anticipated Development(s): The club was granted planning permission for the construction of the new 10,000-seat ground at Cuckoo Farm in late March 2006. If all goes according to plan, the team will start the 2007/08 season at its new ground.

KEY

- **C** Club Offices
- **S** Club Shop
- **E** Entrance(s) for visiting supporters
- **R** Refreshment bars for visiting supporters
- **T** Toilets for visiting supporters

↓ North direction (approx)

- **❶** B1026 Layer Road
- **❷** Town Centre & Colchester Town BR Station (2 miles)
- **❸** Evening Gazette Main Stand
- **❹** Barside Popular Side
- **❺** East Coast Cable Stand

Above: 697285; Right: 697277

A hugely successful season for the now-departed Phil Parkinson and his United team saw the club not only take on Chelsea in the FA Cup at Stamford Bridge, where they acquitted themselves well in an honourable defeat, but also, for the first time in the club's history, achieve promotion to English football's second tier. With three club's battling for the top two spots on the final day of the season, either Southend or Colchester could win the title and either Colchester or Brentford could finish in second place. In the event, Southend's 1-0 home victory over Bristol City combined with Colchester's 0-0 draw away at Yeovil took the title to the coast but the single point was enough to ensure Colchester's promotion irrespective of the result at Bournemouth (where Brentford achieved a 2-2 draw). Away from the league, Phil Parkinson's team showed their potential both in a 2-1 victory at

high-flying Sheffield United in the third round of the FA Cup and in a 3-1 victory over Derby County in the fourth round before succumbing 3-1 at mighty Chelsea in the next round. In what will probably be United's last season at Layer Road, a season of consolidation might be the best that the fans could look forward to but it's hard to escape the conclusion that the team may well struggle to avoid the drop under whoever is appointed to succeed Parkinson.

The Ricoh Arena, Phoenix Way, Foleshill, Coventry CV6 6GE

Telephone: 0870 421 1987
Advance Tickets Tel No: 0870 421 1987
Fax: 0870 421 5073
Web Site: www.ccfc.premiumtv.co.uk
E-mail: info@ccfc.co.uk
League: League Championship
Last Season: 8th (P46; W 16; D 15; L 15; GF 62; GA 65)
Nickname: The Sky Blues
Brief History: Founded 1883 as Singers FC, changed name to Coventry City in 1898. Former grounds: Dowell's Field, Stoke Road Ground and Highfield Road (1899-2005) moved to new ground for start of the 2005/06 season. Record attendance (at Highfield Road): 51,455; (at Ricoh Stadium) 28,120
(Total) Current Capacity: 32,000

Visiting Supporters' Allocation: 3,000 in Jewson South Stand
Club Colours: sky blue shirts, sky blue shorts
Nearest Railway Station: Coventry (three miles)
Parking (Car): As directed
Parking (Coach/Bus): As directed
Police Force and Tel No: West Midlands (02476 539010)
Disabled Visitors' Facilities:
Wheelchairs: tbc
Blind: tbc
Anticipated Development(s): With the completion of the Ricoh Stadium there are no further plans for development at the present time. There is still no news about the construction of a possible station on the Coventry–Nuneaton railway line.

KEY

⬇ North direction (approx)

❶ Judds Lane
❷ Rowley's Green Lane
❸ A444 Phoenix Way
❹ To Coventry city centre and BR railway station (three miles)
❺ Coventry–Nuneaton railway line
❻ To M6 Junction 3 (one mile) and Nuneaton
❼ Marconi West Stand
❽ Coventry Evening Telegraph North Stand
❾ NTL East Stand
❿ Jewson South Stand
⓫ Exhibition hall and planned casino

A season of some progress in the Sky Blues' first campaign at the Ricoh Stadium saw Micky Adams' team improve considerably over the 20th place achieved at the end of the 2004/05 season. Whilst never seriously in the hunt for either automatic promotion or a Play-Off place, in finishing eighth — albeit 12 points off the pace for the all-important sixth place and with a considerably inferior goal difference — City have laid the foundations for a more serious push towards promotion in 2006/07. With both Birmingham City and West Brom relegated the new season offers the potential for more local derbies, games that will have additional spice to them in 2006/07 given that both Birmingham and the Baggies will also have aspirations to make a return to the Premier League. In what has the potential to be a highly competitive League Championship, the Play-Offs are perhaps the best that City fans can look forward to.

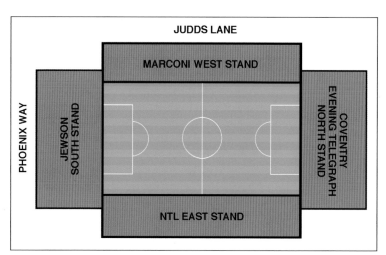

The Alexandra Stadium, Gresty Road, Crewe, Cheshire, CW2 6EB

Tel No: 01270 213014
Advance Tickets Tel No: 01270 252610
Fax: 01270 216320
Website: www.crewealex.premiumtv.co.uk
E-Mail: info@crewealex.net
League: League One
Last Season: 22nd (relegated) (P 46; W 9; D 15; L 22; GF 57; GA 86)
Nickname: The Railwaymen
Brief History: Founded 1877. Former Grounds: Alexandra Recreation Ground (Nantwich Road), Earle Street Cricket Ground, Edleston Road, Old Sheds Fields, Gresty Road (Adjacent to current Ground), moved to current Ground in 1906. Founder members of 2nd Division (1892) until 1896. Founder members of 3rd Division North (1921). Record attendance 20,000
(Total) Current Capacity: 10,100 all seated
Visiting Supporters' Allocation: 1,694 (Blue Bell BMW Stand)

Club Colours: Red shirts, white shorts
Nearest Railway Station: Crewe
Parking (car): There is a car park adjacent to the ground. It should be noted that there is a residents' only scheme in operation in the streets surrounding the ground.
Parking (Coach/Bus): As directed by Police
Police Force and Tel No: Cheshire (01270 500222)
Disabled Visitors' Facilities:
  Wheelchairs: Available on all four sides
  Blind: Commentary available
Anticipated Development(s): The club has long term plans for the construction of a new two-tier stand to replace the Blue Bell (BMW) Stand, although there is no confirmed timescale for the work.

KEY

C Club Offices
S Club Shop
E Entrance(s) for visiting supporters

↑ North direction (approx)

❶ Crewe BR Station
❷ Gresty Road
❸ Gresty Road
❹ A534 Nantwich Road
❺ To A5020 to M6 Junction 16
❻ To M6 Junction 17 [follow directions at roundabout to M6 J16/J17]
❼ Main (Air Products) Stand
❽ Gresty Road (Advance Personnel) Stand
❾ Charles Audi Stand
❿ Ringways Stand (Blue Bell BMW)(away)
⓫ Car Park

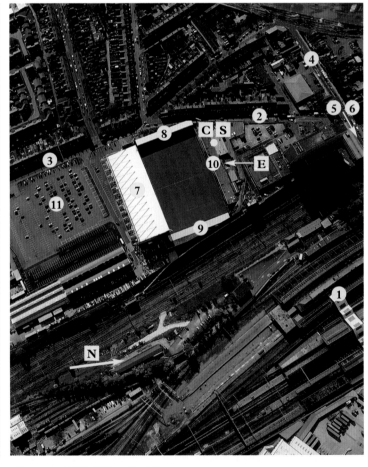

Above: 699095; *Right:* 699100

CREWE ALEXANDRA

Crewe's yo-yo life between the Championship and League One continued with a further relegation that sees Dario Gradi's team drop back to the lower level again. For much of the season it appeared that relegation was inevitable, with the club rooted in the bottom three for the bulk of the campaign. However, a brief improvement towards the end gave hope of a great escape although it was not to be. With the division's worst defensive record it is not hard to identify, ultimately, why the team failed to survive and much, for 2006/07, will depend on the experienced Gradi's ability to resolve these defensive frailties. The defensive frailty was also in evidence in the 5-1 defeat away at League Two Lincoln City in the first round of the Carling cup. The last time that the Railwaymen were relegated, they were to bounce back immediately. As the Football League's longest serving manager with a single club, Gradi has achieved much with the scant resources available to him at Crewe and, this time, it looks as though it will be more difficult to make an immediate return given the potential strength of a number of the other promotion contenders, most notably Huddersfield and Nottingham Forest. Crewe should have the pedigree, however, to achieve a Play-Off place at worst.

Selhurst Park, London, SE25 6PU

Tel No: 020 8768 6000
Advance Tickets Tel No: 08712 000071
Fax: 020 8771 5311
Web Site: www.cpfc.premiumtv.co.uk
E-Mail: info@cpfc.co.uk
Ticket Office/Fax: 020 8653 4708
League: League Championship
Last Season: 6th (P 46; W 21; D 12; L 13; GF 67; GA 48)
Nickname: The Eagles (historically the Glaziers)
Brief History: Founded 1905. Former Grounds: The Crystal Palace (F.A. Cup Finals venue), London County Athletic Ground (Herne Hill), The Nest (Croydon Common Athletic Ground), moved to Selhurst Park in 1924. Founder members 3rd Division (1920). Record attendance 51,482
(Total) Current Capacity: 26,400 all seated
Visiting Supporters' Allocation: Approx 2,000 in Arthur Wait Stand

Club Colours: Blue and red striped shirts, blue shorts
Nearest Railway Station: Selhurst, Norwood Junction and Thornton Heath
Parking (Car): Street parking and Sainsbury's car park
Parking (Coach/Bus): Thornton Heath
Police Force and Tel No: Metropolitan (020 8653 8568)
Disabled Visitors' Facilities:
Wheelchairs: 56 spaces in Arthur Wait and Holmesdale Stands
Blind: Commentary available
Anticipated Development(s): Although the club had plans to reconstruct the Main Stand — indeed had Planning Permission for the work — local opposition has meant that no work has been undertaken. Serious thought is now being given to relocation.

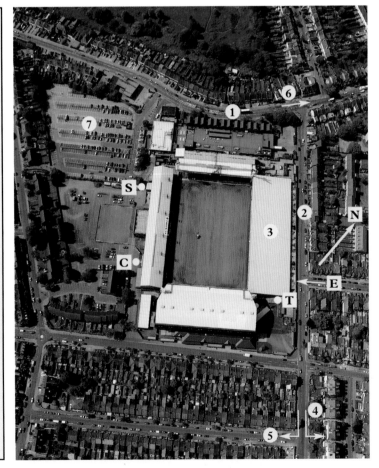

KEY

C Club Offices
S Club Shop
E Entrance(s) for visiting supporters
T Toilets for visiting supporters

↑ North direction (approx)

❶ Whitehorse Lane
❷ Park Road
❸ Arthur Wait Stand Road
❹ Selhurst BR Station (1/2 mile)
❺ Norwood Junction BR Station (1/4 mile)
❻ Thornton Heath BR Station (1/2 mile)
❼ Car Park (Sainsbury's)

Above: 700223; Right: 700220

Relegated along with Norwich and Southampton at the end of the 2004/05 season, Palace under Iain Dowie was the only one of the three relegated teams to make a serious effort at reclaiming a Premier League spot at the first attempt. Whilst never in the hunt for one of the automatic promotion places, a Play-Off position was secured towards the end of the campaign and, by finishing in sixth place, a semi-final against one of the League Championship's surprise packages — Watford — ensued. However, at this point, the wheels went off the Palace machine as a 3-0 home defeat in the first leg proved insurmountable in the return. Eliminated 3-0 on aggregate, Palace face another season in the Championship and, in all probability, the loss of influential players. In late May, Iain Dowie left the club and new boss, the experienced Peter Taylor from Hull City, was quickly appointed. With competition for promotion to the Premier League looking to be even more daunting in 2006/07, perhaps the best that the Selhurst Park faithful can look forward to are the Play-Offs.

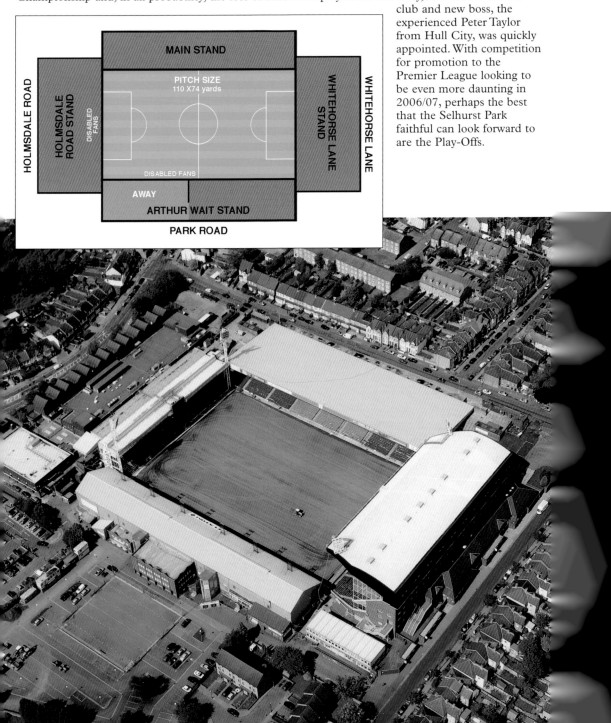

96.6 TFM Darlington Arena, Neasham Road, Darlington DL2 1DL

Tel No: 01325 387000
Advance Tickets Tel No: 0870 027 2949
Fax: 01325 387050
Web Site: www.darlington-fc.premiumtv.co.uk
E-mail: enquiries@darlington-fc.net
League: League Two
Last Season: 8th (P46; W 16; D 15; L 15; GF 58; GA 52)
Nickname: The Quakers
Brief History: Founded 1883. Founder members of 3rd Division (North) 1921. Relegated from 4th Division 1989. Promoted from GM Vauxhall Conference in 1990. Previous Ground: Feethams; moving to Neasham Road in 2003. Record attendance (at Feethams) 21,023; (at Neasham Road) 11,600
(Total) Current Capacity: 27,500
Visiting Supporters' Allocation: 3,000 in East Stand

Club Colours: White and black shirts, black shorts
Nearest Railway Station: Darlington Bank Top
Parking (Car): Spaces available in adjacent car park (£5.00 fee)
Parking (Coach/Bus): As directed
Police Force and Tel No: Durham (01235 467681)
Disabled Visitors Facilities:
  Wheelchairs: 165 places
  Blind: No special facility
Anticipated Developments: With the construction of the new ground, there are no further plans for development as the existing ground's capacity is more than adequate for League Two.

KEY

⬆ North direction (approx)

❶ A66
❷ To Stockton
❸ To A66(M) and A1(M)
❹ Neasham Road
❺ To Darlington town centre and railway station (one mile)
❻ To Neasham
❼ Snipe Lane
❽ East Stand (away)

Above: 695517; *Right:* 695507

Another season of 'What if' for the Quakers saw Dave Hodgson's team again just miss out on the Play-Offs, although in 2005/06 the team's fate was sealed on the penultimate weekend. Again finishing in seventh place, three points below Lincoln, and with an inferior goal difference, Hodgson will be hoping that it will be third time lucky in 2006/07 and that, in the forthcoming season, the Quakers will grab a place in the Play-Offs at least. Away from the now bizarrely named 96.6 TFM Darlington Arena — the new ground seems to have more names in its short life than your editor has had hot dinners in the past month — there was sad news about the club's old ground, Feethams, which succumbed to the demolition contractors in early 2006.

NORTH STAND

PITCH SIZE
110 X 74 yards

WEST STAND

EAST STAND

SOUTH STAND

NEASHAM ROAD

Pride Park, Derby, Derbyshire DE24 8XL

Tel No: 0870 444 1884
Advance Tickets Tel No: 0870 444 1884
Fax: 01332 667540
Web Site: www.dcfc.co.uk
E-Mail: derby.county@dcfc.co.uk
League: League Championship
Last Season: 20th (P46; W 10; D 20; L 16; GF 53; GA 67)
Nickname: The Rams
Brief History: Founded 1884. Former grounds: The Racecourse Ground, the Baseball Ground (1894-1997), moved to Pride Park 1997. Founder members of the Football League (1888). Record capacity at the Baseball Ground: 41,826; at Pride Park: 33,597
(Total) Current Capacity: 33,597
Visiting Supporters' Allocation: 4,800 maximum in the South Stand

Club Colours: White shirts and black shorts
Nearest Railway Station: Derby
Parking (Car): 2,300 places at the ground designated for season ticket holders. Also two 1,000 car parks on the A6/A52 link road. No on-street parking
Parking (Coach/Bus): As directed
Police Force and Tel No: Derbyshire (01332 290100)
Disabled Visitors' Facilities:
　Wheelchairs: 70 home/30 away spaces
　Blind: Commentary available
Anticipated Development(s): There are no definite plans for the further development of Pride Park following the completion of the southwest corner.

KEY

C Club Offices
S Club Shop
E Entrance(s) for visiting supporters

↑ North direction (approx)

❶ To Derby Midland BR station
❷ North Stand
❸ Toyota West Stand
❹ South (McArthur Glen) Stand (away)
❺ Bombardier East Stand
❻ Derwent Parade
❼ To A52/M1
❽ To City Centre and A6
❾ A52

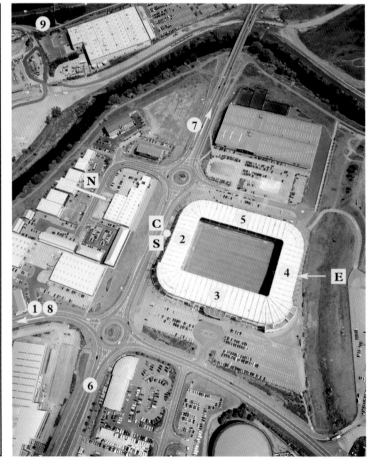

Above: 697495; *Right:* 697485

Following the club's success at the end of the 2004/05 season in reaching fourth place and the Play-Offs, there was considerable expectation that Phil Brown's Derby side would again feature in the battle for a return to the Premier League. However, this expectation were quickly extinguished as the season saw the Rams more interested in events at Crewe and Millwall rather than at Reading or Sheffield United. Appointed only in the summer of 2005, Phil Brown's reign as manager at Pride Park came to an end at the end of January following a dismal run in the league, which left the Rams in 19th place, and a 3-1 defeat away at League One side Colchester United in the fourth round of the FA Cup (which had followed an earlier defeat by a lower league team in the Carling Cup when League two side Grimsby Town had won 1-0 at Pride Park in the first round). The club appointed Terry Westley as caretaker, before confirming him as manager for the remainder of the season at the end of February. The League Championship's draw specialists — no fewer than 20 matches resulted in the points being shared — County were at one stage in serious danger of being sucked into the relegation battle. In the event, whilst 20th was a poor result, it was eight points above relegated Crewe in 22nd. In early June it was announced that ex-Preston boss, Billy Davies (who'd again taken the Lancashire side to the Play-Offs) would be taking over as manager. Having guided unfancied Preston to two successive Play-Off semi-finals, Davies has the pedigree to restore the glory days to Pride Park, but a top half finish is perhaps the best that fans can look forward to.

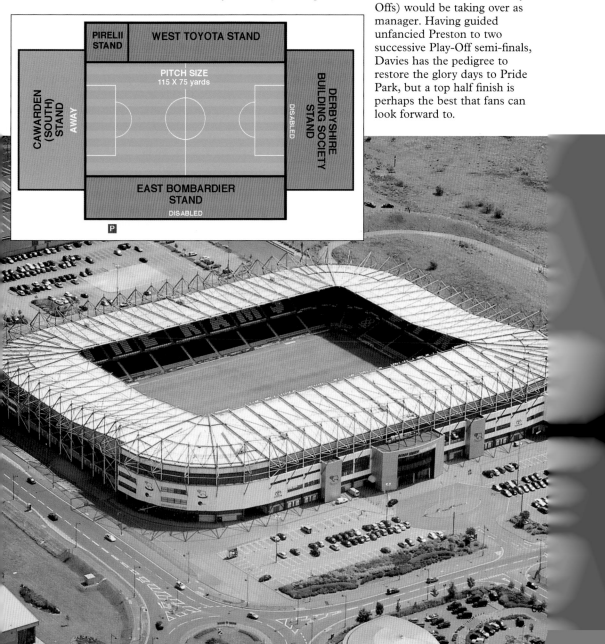

Lakeside Stadium, Lakeside Boulevard, Doncaster

Tel No: 01302 539441*
Advance Tickets Tel No: 01302 539441*
Fax: 01302 5396798*
* These are the numbers for Belle Vue and may change with the relocation to the new ground
Web Site:
www.doncasterroversfc.premiumtv.co.uk
E-mail: info@doncasterroversfc.co.uk
League: League One
Last Season: 8th (P 46; W 20; D9; L 17; GF 55; GA 51)
Nickname: The Rovers
Brief History: Founded 1879. Former grounds: Town Moor, Belle Vue (not later ground), Deaf school Playing field (later name Intake Ground), Bennetthorpe, Belle Vue (1922-2006). Returned to Football League after a five-year absence in 2003. Record attendance (at Belle Vue) 37,149

(Total) Current Capacity: 15,000
Visiting Supporters' Allocation: tbc
Club Colours: Red and white shirts, red shorts
Nearest Railway Station: Doncaster
Parking (Car): 1,000 place car park at ground
Parking (Coach/Bus): As directed
Other Clubs Sharing Ground: Doncaster Dragons RLFC and Doncaster Belles Ladies FC
Police Force and Tel No: South Yorkshire (01302 366744)
Disabled Visitors' Facilities:
Wheelchairs: tbc
Blind: tbc
Anticipated Development(s): The club is planning to move to this new ground early in the 2006/07 season. Costing £32 million, the new stadium has been designed to permit expansion to a capacity of 20,000 if required.

KEY

⬆ North direction (approx)

❶ Lakeside Boulevard
❷ A6182 White Rose Way
❸ To Doncaster town centre and railway station
❹ To Junction 3 M18
❺ Lakeside Stadium
❻ Site of 1,000 place car park
❼ Future athletics ground

DONCASTER ROVERS

Above: 699881; *Right:* 699891

Another successful season at Belle Vue, the club's last full campaign at this venerable ground, saw Dave Penney's team in with a shout of the Play-Offs right until the final weekend of the season. On the last Saturday, three teams — Rovers, Forest and Swansea — all had hopes of the all-important sixth position. However, for Rovers to pip the other two teams needed them to beat Tranmere at Prenton Park and hope that both Forest and Swansea lost. In the event, a 2-0 win at Tranmere was not enough to counter Swansea's emphatic 4-0 win at Chesterfield and Forest's 1-1 draw at Bradford. As a result, Rovers new ground, due to open during the course of the 2006/07 season, will witness League One

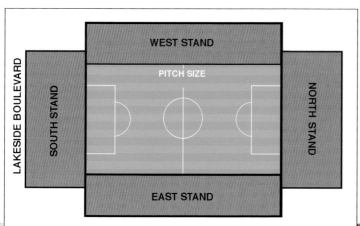

football initially. It wasn't just in the league that Dave Penney's team impressed; victories over Manchester City (on penalties) and Aston Villa (3-0) set up a quarter final in the Carling cup with Arsenal (which the Gunners were lucky to scrape through on penalties after the game had ended 2-2 AET). However, provided that the progress on the field can be maintained and match the investment off it, then Rovers should again be in the hunt for the Play-Offs at worst.

Goodison Park, Goodison Road, Liverpool, L4 4EL

Tel No: 0870 442 1878
Advance Tickets Tel No: 0870 442 1878
Fax: 0151 286 9112
Web Site: www.evertonfc.com
E-Mail: everton@evertonfc.com
League: F.A. Premier
Last Season: 11th (P 38; W 14; D 8; L 16; GF 34; GA 49)
Nickname: The Toffees
Brief History: Founded 1879 as St. Domingo, changed to Everton in 1880. Former grounds: Stanley Park, Priory Road and Anfield (Liverpool F.C. Ground), moved to Goodison Park in 1892. Founder-members Football League (1888). Record attendance 78,299
(Total) Current Capacity: 40,569 all seated
Visiting Supporters' Allocation: 3,000 (part of Bullens Road Stand) maximum
Club Colours: Blue and white shirts, white shorts
Nearest Railway Station: Kirkdale

Parking (Car): Corner of Utting Avenue and Priory Road
Parking (Coach/Bus): Priory Road
Police Force and Tel No: Merseyside (0151 709 6010)
Disabled Visitors' Facilities:
Wheelchairs: Bullens Road Stand
Blind: Commentary available
Anticipated Development(s): Having abandoned earlier proposals to relocate to a new stadium in the King's Dock area, the club is still keen to move from Goodison and is now investigating the possibility of constructing a 55,000-seat stadium in the Central Docks area. This is, however, only a tentative proposal at this stage and much will depend on getting the funding in place. Another recent proposal is for the club to share Liverpool FC's planned new ground. Expect Everton to remain at Goodison for probably two or three seasons at least.

KEY

C Club Offices
S Club Shop
E Entrance(s) for visiting supporters
R Refreshment bars for visiting supporters
T Toilets for visiting supporters

↑ North direction (approx)

❶ A580 Walton Road
❷ Bullen Road
❸ Goodison Road
❹ Car Park
❺ Liverpool Lime Street BR Station (2 miles)
❻ To M57 Junction 2, 4 and 5
❼ Stanley Park
❽ Bullens Road Stand
❾ Park Stand
❿ Main Stand
⓫ Gwladys Stand

Above: 700047; *Right:* 700053

EVERTON

Following the success at the end of the 2004/05 season, when Everton had finished in fourth place pipping Liverpool to automatic entry to the Champions League, optimism was high at Goodison Park that the new season would see further progress on the field. Whilst it was unlikely that the team would challenge Chelsea for the top, a top-four position should certainly have been achievable. In the event, 2005/06 was to prove a huge disappointment. Failure to make it to the group stages of the Champions League was compounded by an abysmal start to the league campaign; indeed for a period it looked as though relegation was starting to stalk the corridors at Goodison. However, form picked up and ultimately the club was able to pull away from the drop zone, finishing in 11th place.

Whilst this was poor in comparison with the previous season it did represent a considerable improvement on earlier in the season. Under David Moyes, Everton seem to alternate; one poor season follows one good one and, on that basis, the club is due a good one. Whilst it's unlikely that the club can challenge for a top-four spot again, a decent top half finish — with the outside possibility of the UEFA Cup spots — should be possible.

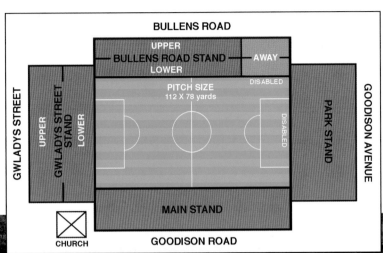

BULLENS ROAD

UPPER
BULLENS ROAD STAND — AWAY
LOWER

DISABLED

PITCH SIZE
112 X 78 yards

DISABLED

GWLADYS STREET

UPPER GWLADYS STREET STAND LOWER

PARK STAND

GOODISON AVENUE

MAIN STAND

CHURCH

GOODISON ROAD

Craven Cottage, Stevenage Road, Fulham, London SW6 6HH

Club Offices: Fulham FC Training Ground, Motspur Park, New Malden, Surrey KT3 6PT

Tel No: 0870 442 1222

Advance Tickets Tel No: 0870 442 1234

Fax: 020 8442 0236

Web-site: www.fulhamfc.com

E-mail: enquiries@fulhamfc.com

League: F.A. Premier

Last Season: 12th (P38; W 14; D 6; L 18; GF 48; GA 58)

Nickname: The Cottagers

Brief History: Founded in 1879 at St. Andrews Fulham, changed name to Fulham in 1898. Former grounds: Star Road, Ranelagh Club, Lillie Road, Eel Brook Common, Purer's Cross, Barn Elms, Half Moon (Wasps Rugby Football Ground), Craven Cottage (from 1894), moved to Loftus Road 2002 and returned to Craven Cottage for start of the 2004/05 season. Record Attendance: Craven Cottage (49,335)

(Total) Current Capacity: 22,480 (all seated)

Visiting Supporters' Allocation: 3,000 in Putney End

Club Colours: White shirts, black shorts

Nearest Railway Station: Putney Bridge (Tube)

Parking (Car): Street parking

Parking(Coach/Bus): Stevenage Road

Police Force and Tel No: Metropolitan (020 7741 6212)

Disabled Visitors' Facilities:

   Wheelchairs: Main Stand and Hammersmith End

   Blind: No special facility

Anticipated Development(s): Now restored to its traditional home at Craven Cottage, the club is looking either to further develop the ground with a view to obtaining an increased capacity. The most likely route is via the construction of corner infill stands and the rebuilding of the existing stands. There is, however, no confirmed timescale for this work.

KEY

E Entrance(s) for visiting supporters

R Refreshment bars for visiting supporters

T Toilets for visiting supporters

↑ North direction (approx)

❶ River Thames

❷ Stevenage Road

❸ Finlay Street

❹ Putney Bridge Tube Station (0.5 mile)

❺ Putney End (away)

❻ Riverside Stand

❼ Main Stand

❽ Hammersmith End

❾ Craven Cottage

Above: 700230; *Right:* 700228

FULHAM

If football is a game of two halves, Fulham's season was one of two types of venue: at home the Cottagers were well nigh invincible, dropping only some 16 points out of the 57 available; away from home, however, it was a completely different matter with the club gaining only seven points all season (and only winning once in its travels — the final away game of the season at Manchester City). Given the club's home form (ironic considering that the team had been defeated 2-1 by League Two side Leyton Orient in the third round of the FA Cup at Craven Cottage), Chris Coleman's team was never likely to get sucked into the relegation battle, but its failure to take many points away from Craven Cottage against struggling teams is a potential worry for the future, particularly as the club's finances are not the strongest in the Premier League. In Coleman, the club has a manager who has proved himself capable of marshalling his resources to keep Fulham in the Premier League; with three overtly 'weak' teams coming up the team should again ensure Premier League survival but until it can start to perform away from home, the club will always be in the wrong half of the table.

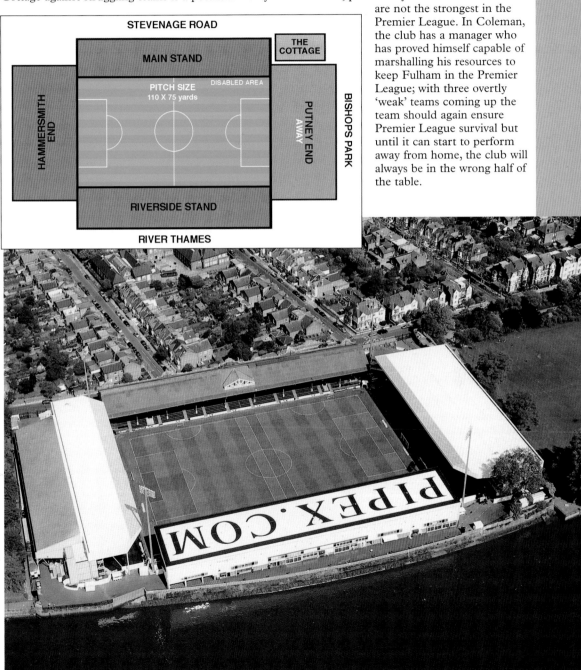

Priestfield Stadium, Redfern Avenue, Gillingham, Kent, ME7 4DD

Tel No: 01634 300000
Advance Tickets Tel No: 01634 300000
Fax: 01634 850986
Web Site: www.gillinghamfootballclub.premiumtv.co.uk
E-mail: info@priestfield.com
League: League One
Last Season: 14th (P46; W 16; D 12; L 18; GF 50; GA 64)
Nickname: The Gills
Brief History: Founded 1893, as New Brompton, changed name to Gillingham in 1913. Founder-members Third Division (1920). Lost Football League status (1938), re-elected to Third Division South (1950). Record attendance 23,002
(Total) Current Capacity: 11,582 (all seated)
Visiting Supporters' Allocation: 1,500 (in Gillingham (Brian Moore Stand) End)
Club Colours: Blue and black hooped shirts, blue shorts

Nearest Railway Station: Gillingham
Parking (Car): Street parking
Parking (Coach/Bus): As directed by Police
Police Force and Tel No: Kent (01634 234488)
Disabled Visitors' Facilities:
  Wheelchairs: Redfern Avenue (Main) Stand
  Blind: No special facility
Anticipated Development(s): The old open Town End Terrace was demolished during 2003 and replaced by a new temporary open stand. Planning Permission was granted in 2003 for the construction of a new 3,500-seat stand, to be named after noted fan the late Brian Moore, although work has yet to commence. Despite the investment at Priestfield, however, the club is investigating, in conjunction with the local council, the possibility of constructing a new stadium at Temple Marsh.

KEY

E Entrance(s) for visiting supporters

↑ North direction (approx)

❶ Redfern Avenue
❷ Toronto Road
❸ Gordon Road
❹ Gillingham BR station (¼ mile)
❺ Gordon Street Stand
❻ New two-tier Main (Medway) Stand
❼ New Rainham End Stand
❽ Gillingham End; uncovered seating (away)

GILLINGHAM

76

Above: 697309; *Right:* 697302

In mid-November, with the Gills rooted in the League One relegation mire after a series of poor results and having suffered defeat 3-2 away at non-league Burscough in the First Round of the FA Cup, manager Neale Cooper resigned. He was replaced as caretaker by assistant Ronnie Jepson, who was subsequently confirmed as manager on a permanent basis. Off the field, at the same time, chairman Paul Scally was battling to keep the team out of Administration. Under Jepson's the club's playing fortunes improved immeasurably, with, at one stage, a run of six straight wins. Ultimately finishing in 14th position was a dramatic improvement on what had seemed likely earlier in the season and, with Jepson having been told that he can add to his squad during the close season, there will be considerable optimism at Priestfield that the Gills can reclaim the Championship spot that they surrendered at the end of the 2004/05 season.

Blundell Park, Cleethorpes, DN35 7PY

Tel No: 01472 605050
Advance Tickets Tel No: 01472 605050
Fax: 01472 693665
Web Site: www.grimsby-townfc.premiumtv.co.uk
E-Mail: enquiries@gtfc.co.uk
League: League Two
Last Season: 4th (P 46; W 22; D 12; L 12; GF 64; GA 44)
Nickname: The Mariners
Brief History: Founded in 1878, as Grimsby Pelham, changed name to Grimsby Town in 1879. Former Grounds: Clee Park (two adjacent fields) and Abbey Park, moved to Blundell Park in 1899. Founder-members 2nd Division (1892). Record attendance 31,651
(Total) Current Capacity: 9,000 (all seated)
Visiting Supporters' Allocation: 2,000 in Osmond Stand

Club Colours: Black and white striped shirts, black shorts
Nearest Railway Station: Cleethorpes
Parking (Car): Street parking
Parking (Coach/Bus): Harrington Street
Police Force and Tel No: Humberside (01472 359171)
Disabled Visitors' Facilities:
Wheelchairs: Harrington Street (Main) Stand
Blind: Commentary available
Anticipated Development(s): In late January it was announced that the club had applied for planning permission to construct a new 20,000-seat ground, to be called the Conoco Stadium, at Great Coates. If all goes according to plan, the new ground would be available for the start of the 2008/09 season.

GRIMSBY TOWN

KEY

C Club Offices
S Club Shop
E Entrance(s) for visiting supporters
R Refreshment bars for visiting supporters
T Toilets for visiting supporters

↑ North direction (approx)

❶ A180 Grimsby Road
❷ Cleethorpes BR Station (1½ miles)
❸ To Grimsby and M180 Junction 5
❹ Harrington Street
❺ Constitutional Avenue
❻ Humber Estuary

Above: 697766; *Right:* 697756

If a week is a long time in politics then a minute can represent an eternity in football as fans of the Mariners learnt at the end of the 2005/06 season. With a minute to go, Grimsby were leading 1-0 at home to Northampton and Leyton Orient were drawing 2-2 at Oxford United; if results stayed that way then Town were on their way back to League One. However, in the space of the final minute of the league season all that changed. Northampton equalised at Blundell Park and Orient scored a winner at the Kassam Stadium. The result was delirium for Orient fans and despair in Grimsby. However, optimism was restored after a two-leg victory over rival Lincoln City saw Town head to the Millennium Stadium for a final against Cheltenham Town. However, a 1-0 defeat means that Grimsby face the 2006/07 season again in League Two. In a season of much disappointment there was one considerable success: the run in the Carling Cup where a 1-0 victory away at Derby County was followed by a 1-0 victory over Premier League team Tottenham Hotspur in the second round. Shortly after the Play-Off defeat it was announced that Russell Slade was leaving the club; new boss Graham Rodger, promoted from being Slade's assistant, will have the basis of a squad capable of chasing automatic promotion but again the Play-Offs may be the best that the club can aspire to.

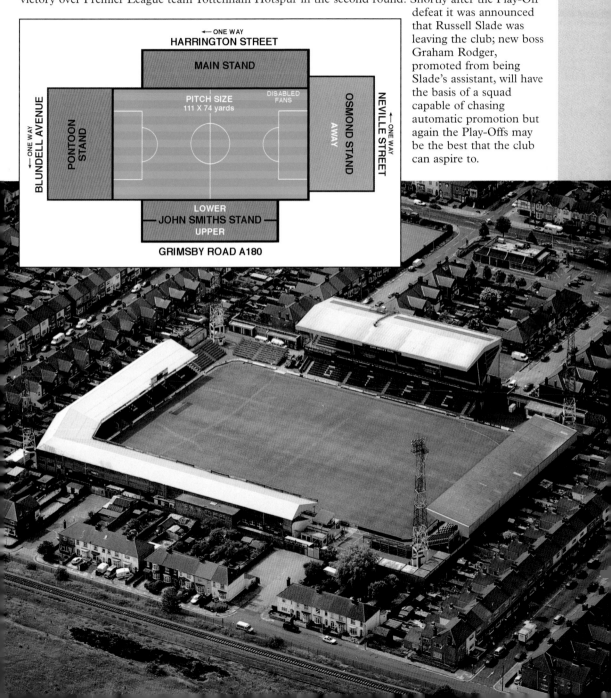

Victoria Park, Clarence Road, Hartlepool, TS24 8BZ

Tel No: 01429 272584
Advance Tickets Tel No: 01429 272584
Fax: 01429 863007
Web Site: www.hartlepoolunited.premiumtv.co.uk
E-Mail: enquiries@hartlepoolunited.co.uk
Fax: 01429 863007
League: League Two
Last Season: 21st (relegated) (P 46; W 11; D 17; L 18; GF 44; GA 59)
Nickname: The Pool
Brief History: Founded 1908 as Hartlepools United, changed to Hartlepool (1968) and to Hartlepool United in 1977. Founder-members 3rd Division (1921). Record attendance 17,426
(Total) Current Capacity: 7,629 (3,966 seated)
Visiting Supporters' Allocation: 1,000 (located in Rink Stand)
Club Colours: Blue and white striped shirts, blue shorts

Nearest Railway Station: Hartlepool Church Street
Parking (Car): Street parking and rear of clock garage
Parking (Coach/Bus): As directed
Police Force and Tel No: Cleveland (01429 221151
Disabled Visitors' Facilities:
Wheelchairs: Cyril Knowles Stand and Rink End
Blind: Commentary available
Anticipated Development(s): The plans for the redevelopment of the Millhouse Stand are still progressing, although there is now no definite timescale. When this work does commence, the ground's capacity will be reduced to 5,000 temporarily.

KEY

C Club Offices
S Club Shop
E Entrance(s) for visiting supporters

↑ North direction (approx)

❶ A179 Clarence Road
❷ Hartlepool Church Street BR Station
❸ Marina Way
❹ Site of former Greyhound Stadium
❺ To Middlesbrough A689 & A1(M)
❻ To A19 North
❼ Rink End Stand

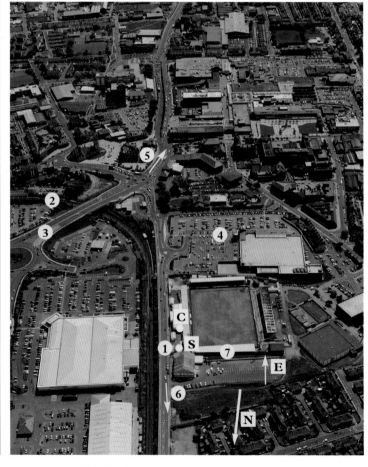

Above: 700403; *Right:* 700411

HARTLEPOOL UNITED

With the club having failed to win any of its preceding nine games, having also been knocked out of the FA Cup in the second round by non-league Tamworth, and hovering in the League One drop zone following a 3-0 defeat against fellow strugglers Blackpool, manager Martin Scott was suspended as a result of an incident in the dressing room in early February and the following week departed from the club 'by mutual consent'. He was replaced as caretaker by Paul Stephenson who was later confirmed in the position until the end of the season with ex-boss Chris Turner brought in as Director of Sport. Unfortunately, Stephenson wasn't able to arrest the club's decline, although relegation was not confirmed until the final day when, despite drawing at home against Port Vale, Rotherham's draw at Millmoor against fellow strugglers Milton Keynes Dons secured League One football for the South Yorkshire team. At the end of the game, Stephenson commented that one of the factors in the club's relegation was its inability to convert the many chances it created — a fact confirmed by the total of only 44 league goals scored all season (the lowest in League One). New manager Danny Wilson, who previously managed Milton Keynes Dons, will have his work cut to see United as a serious promotion candidate unless this weakness is addressed; perhaps a Play-Off place at best is the most that fans can look forward to.

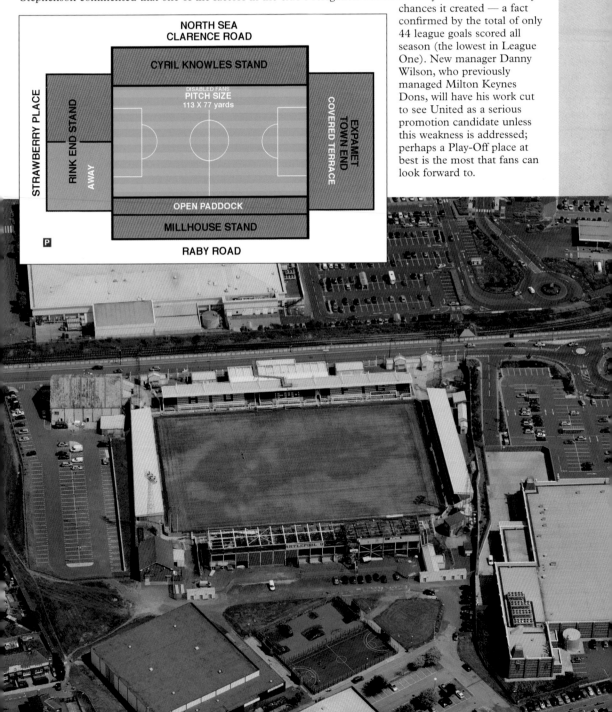

NORTH SEA
CLARENCE ROAD

CYRIL KNOWLES STAND

DISABLED FANS
PITCH SIZE
113 X 77 yards

STRAWBERRY PLACE

RINK END STAND

AWAY

EXPAMET
TOWN END
COVERED TERRACE

OPEN PADDOCK

MILLHOUSE STAND

RABY ROAD

Edgar Street, Hereford, HR4 9JU

Telephone: 01432 276666
Advance Tickets Tel No: 01432 276666
Fax: 01432 341359
Web Site: www.herefordunited.co.uk
E-mail: hufc1939@hotmail.com
League: League Two
Last Season: 2nd (promoted via the Play Offs from the Conference) (P 42; W 22; D 14; L 6; GF 59; GA 33)
Nickname: Bulls
Brief History: Founded 1924; first elected to the Football League 1972; relegated to the Conference 1997; promoted through the Play-Offs at the end of 2005/06. Record attendance 18,115

(Total) Current Capacity: 8,843 (1,761 seated)
Visiting Supporters' Allocation: tbc (Blackfriars Street End)
Club Colours: White shirts, white shorts
Nearest Railway Station: Hereford
Parking (Car): Merton Meadow and Edgar Street
Parking (Coach/Bus): Cattle Market
Police Force and Tel No: West Mercia (08457 444888)
Disabled Visitors' Facilities:
　Wheelchairs: Edgar Street (limited)
　Blind: Commentary available
Anticipated Development(s):

HEREFORD UNITED

KEY

- **C** Club Offices
- **S** Club Shop
- **E** Entrance(s) for visiting supporters
- **R** Refreshment bars for visiting supporters
- **T** Toilets for visiting supporters

⬆ North direction (approx)

- ❶ A49(T) Edgar Street
- ❷ Blackfriars Street
- ❸ Len Weston Stand
- ❹ Merton Meadow Stand
- ❺ Merton Meadow Terrace
- ❻ Blackfriars Street End
- ❼ To Town Centre and Hereford BR Station
- ❽ B4359 Windermere Street

Above: 700427; *Right:* 700436

After an absence of almost a decade and several near misses in previous seasons, Graham Turner's Hereford United return to the Football League after a successful season in the Conference saw the Bulls finish in second place behind Accrington Stanley and thus enter the Play-Offs. Victory over another famous ex-league team, Halifax Town, in the Final at the Walkers Stadium brings league football back to Edgar Street and the opportunity to renew local rivalry with neighbouring Shrewsbury Town. As with other teams promoted from the Conference, United may well not find a huge difference in quality and should certainly be able to retain its league status by the end of the campaign. In terms of consolidation, perhaps a position in mid-table would be the most likely result but as other promoted teams have shown in recent seasons — most notably Doncaster and Carlisle — promotion is by no means an impossibility.

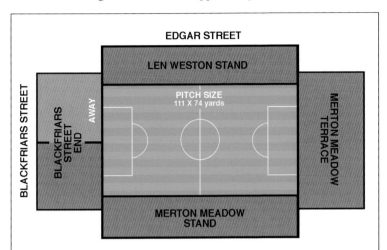

EDGAR STREET

LEN WESTON STAND

BLACKFRIARS STREET

BLACKFRIARS STREET END

AWAY

PITCH SIZE
111 X 74 yards

MERTON MEADOW TERRACE

MERTON MEADOW STAND

The Galpharm Stadium, Leeds Road, Huddersfield, HD1 6PX

Tel No: 0870 444 4677
Advance Tickets Tel No: 0870 444 4552
Fax: 01484 484101
Web Site: www.htafc.premiumtv.co.uk
E-Mail: info@htafc.com
League: League One
Last Season: 4th (P46; W 19; D 16; L 11; GF 72; GA 59)
Nickname: The Terriers
Brief History: Founded 1908, elected to Football League in 1910. First Club to win the Football League Championship three years in succession. Moved from Leeds Road ground to Kirklees (Alfred McAlpine) Stadium 1994/95 season. Record attendance (Leeds Road) 67,037; Galpharm Stadium: 23,678
(Total) Current Capacity: 24,500 (all seated)
Visiting Supporters' Allocation: 4,037 (all seated)

Club Colours: Blue and white striped shirts, white shorts
Nearest Railway Station: Huddersfield
Parking (Car): Car parks (pre-sold) adjacent to ground
Parking (Coach/Bus): Car parks adjacent to ground
Other Clubs Sharing Ground: Huddersfield Giants RLFC
Police Force and Tel No: West Yorkshire (01484 422122)
Disabled Visitors' Facilities:
  Wheelchairs: Three sides of Ground, at low levels and raised area, including toilet access
  Blind: Area for partially sighted with Hospital Radio commentary
Anticipated Development(s): With completion of the new North Stand, work on the Galpharm Stadium is over.

HUDDERSFIELD TOWN

KEY

C Club Offices
S Club Shop
E Entrance(s) for visiting supporters

⬆ North direction (approx)

❶ To Leeds and M62 Junction 25
❷ A62 Leeds Road
❸ To Huddersfield BR station (1¼ miles)
❹ Disabled parking
❺ North Stand
❻ St Andrews pay car park
❼ Coach park
❽ South (Pink Link) Stand (away)

Above: 700079; *Right:* 700085

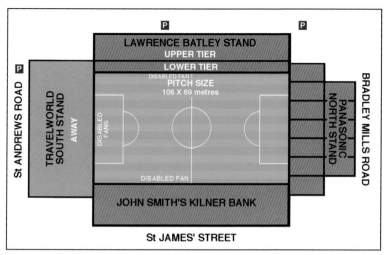

St ANDREWS ROAD

P

LAWRENCE BATLEY STAND

UPPER TIER

LOWER TIER

DISABLED FAN

PITCH SIZE
106 X 69 metres

TRAVELWORLD
SOUTH STAND

AWAY

DISABLED
FANS

DISABLED FAN

JOHN SMITH'S KILNER BANK

St JAMES' STREET

BRADLEY MILLS ROAD

PANASONIC
NORTH STAND

The Terriers, like Brentford, must be cursing the luck of the Play-Offs. Having been in the hunt for one of the automatic promotion spots for virtually all of the season, it was only the penultimate weekend that consigned Peter Jackson's team to the Play-Offs. By finishing fourth, the club faced neighbours Barnsley in a crunch semi-final for the opportunity of playing Swansea at the Millennium Stadium. A 1-0 victory at Oakwell seemed to have given Town the edge but a 3-1 home defeat to Andy Ritchie's team consigns Town to another season of League One football. Provided that Jackson can retain the majority of his squad as the basis for next season then Town should again feature in the race for automatic promotion.

Kingston Communications Stadium, Walton Street, Hull, East Yorkshire HU3 6HU

Tel No: 0870 837 0003
Advance Tickets Tel No: 0870 837 0004
Fax: 01482 304882
Web Site: www.hullcityafc.premiumtv.co.uk
E-mail: info@hulltigers.com
League: League Championship
Last Season: 18th (P46; W 12; D 16; L 18; GF 49; GA 55)
Nickname: The Tigers
Brief History: Founded 1904. Former grounds: The Boulevard (Hull Rugby League Ground), Dairycoates, Anlaby Road Cricket Circle (Hull Cricket Ground), Anlaby Road, Boothferry Park (from 1946). Moved to Kingston Communications Stadium in late 2002. Record attendance (at Boothferry Park) 55,019; (at Kingston Communications Stadium) 25,280
(Total) Current Capacity: 25,504 (all-seated)
Visiting Supporters' Allocation: 4,000 all-seated in North Stand
Club Colours: Amber and black striped shirts, black shorts

Nearest Railway Station: Hull Paragon
Parking (Car): There are 1,800 spaces on the Walton Street Fairground for use on match days
Parking (Coach/Bus): As directed
Other Clubs Sharing Ground: Hull RLFC
Police Force and Tel No: Humberside (01482 220148)
Disabled Visitors' facilities:
  Wheelchairs: c300 places
  Blind: Contact club for details
Anticipated Development(s): The club moved into the new Kingston Communication Stadium towards the end of 2002. The ground is shared with Hull RLFC. The total cost of the 25,504-seat ground was £44million. The West Stand is provided with two tiers and there are plans for the construction of a second tier on the East and South Stands, taking the capacity to 34,000, if required.

KEY

⬆ North direction (approx)

❶ A1105 Anlaby Road
❷ Arnold Lane
❸ West Stand
❹ East Stand
❺ Walton Street
❻ To city centre and railway station
❼ Car parks
❽ Railway line towards Scarborough
❾ Railway line towards Leeds
❿ A1105 westwards towards A63 and M62

Above: 695565; *Right:* 695561

Promoted at the end of 2004/05, the priority for Peter Taylor's team was to ensure that it secured its League Championship position and, in finishing in 18th place, the team certainly achieved that. Never really threatened with an immediate return to League One, unlike fellow promoted team Sheffield Wednesday, the Tigers ultimately finished a comfortable 10 points above relegated Crewe. Away from the league, one disappointment was a 2-1 defeat away at Blackpool in the Carling Cup. However, whilst the arrival of three relatively weak teams from League One at the end of 2005/06 should make the team's Championship status more secure, there is one minor fly in the ointment — the move of Peter Taylor to take over at Crystal Palace. Under Taylor, the club has laid the foundations to become a secure Championship team — perhaps not quite good enough to challenge yet for a place in the Premier League but certainly more than capable of reaching a mid-table position — and the challenge for his successor — Phil Parkinson — will be to maintain this progress on the field.

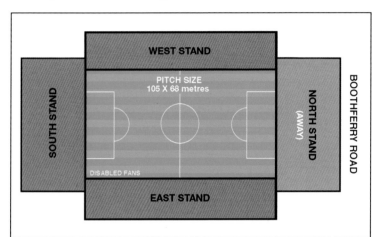

WEST STAND

PITCH SIZE
105 X 68 metres

SOUTH STAND

NORTH STAND
(AWAY)

BOOTHFERRY ROAD

DISABLED FANS

EAST STAND

Portman Road, Ipswich, IP1 2DA

Tel No: 01473 400500
Advance Tickets Tel No: 0870 1110555
Fax: 01473 400040
Web Site: www.itfc.premiumtv.co.uk
E-Mail: enquiries@itfc.co.uk
League: League Championship
Last Season: 15th (P 46; W 14; D 14; L 18; GF 53; GA 66)
Nickname: Tractorboys
Brief History: Founded 1887 as Ipswich Association F.C., changed to Ipswich Town in 1888. Former Grounds: Broom Hill & Brookes Hall, moved to Portman Road in 1888. Record attendance 38,010
(Total) Current Capacity: 30,311 all seated
Visiting Supporters' Allocation: 2,280 all seated in Cobbold Stand

Club Colours: Blue shirts, white shorts
Nearest Railway Station: Ipswich
Parking (Car): Portman Road, Portman Walk & West End Road
Parking (Coach/Bus): West End Road
Police Force and Tel No: Suffolk (01473 611611)
Disabled Visitors' Facilities:
  Wheelchairs: Lower Britannia Stand
  Blind: Commentary available
Anticipated Development(s): The new Greene King (South) Stand has been followed by the construction of the new two-tier, 7,035-seat, North Stand, which was initially delayed as a result of legal action. The completion of the two stands takes Portman Road's capacity to more than 30,000.

	KEY
C	Club Offices
E	Entrance(s) for visiting supporters
R	Refreshment bars for visiting supporters
T	Toilets for visiting supporters

↑ North direction (approx)

❶ A137 West End Road
❷ Sir Alf Ramsay Way
❸ Portman Road
❹ Princes Street
❺ To Ipswich BR Station
❻ Car Parks
❼ Cobbold Stand
❽ Britannia Stand
❾ North Stand
❿ Greene King (South) Stand

Above: 699778; *Right:* 699784

A disappointing season for the Tractorboys given that they were considered by many to be potential candidates for promotion. A lacklustre campaign — perhaps epitomised by the 2-0 home defeat by League One Yeovil Town in the first round of the Carling Cup — resulted in the team finishing in 15th position in the League Championship and ultimately cost manager Joe Royle his job when, after the end of the season, it was announced that he had left the club by mutual agreement. New manager — Jim Magilton (who retired from playing at the end of the 2005/06 season and who will be the youngest manager in the Championship) — will have his work cut out to achieve anything better than a top half finish in 2006/07.

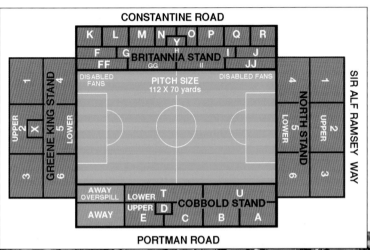

Elland Road, Leeds, LS11 0ES

Tel No: 0113 367 6000
Advance Tickets Tel No: 0845 121 1992
Fax: 0113 367 6050
Web Site: www.leedsunited.com
E-mail: admin@leedsunited.com
League: League Championship
Last Season: 5th (P 46; W 21; D 15; L 10; GF 57; GA 38)
Nickname: United
Brief History: Founded 1919, formed from the former 'Leeds City' Club, who were disbanded following expulsion from the Football League in October 1919. Joined Football League in 1920. Record attendance 57,892
(Total) Current Capacity: 40,296 (all seated)
Visiting Supporters' Allocation: 1,725 in South East Corner (can be increased to 3,662 in South Stand if necessary)

Club Colours: White shirts, white shorts
Nearest Railway Station: Leeds City
Parking (Car): Car parks adjacent to ground
Parking (Coach/Bus): As directed by Police
Police Force and Tel No: West Yorkshire (0113 243 5353)
Disabled Visitors' Facilities:
Wheelchairs: West Stand and South Stand
Blind: Commentary available
Anticipated Development(s): Although the club had proposals for relocation to a new 50,000-seat stadium costing £60 million to be constructed close to the A1/M1 link road, given the club's high profile financial problems and recent relegation to the League Championship, it is unclear whether this work will proceed. The club has sold the Elland Road site and leased it back.

KEY

C Club Offices
S Club Shop
E Entrance(s) for visiting supporters

⬆ North direction (approx)

❶ M621
❷ M621 Junction 2
❸ A643 Elland Road
❹ Lowfields Road
❺ To A58
❻ City Centre and BR station
❼ To M62 and M1

Above: 700145; *Right:* 700135

In United's second season back in the Championship, Kevin Blackwall's team looked certain of a Play-Off position for most of the campaign; indeed, such was Sheffield United's loss of form mid-season that it looked at one stage that either United or Watford could have been in a position to snatch the second automatic promotion spot. In the event, both Leeds and Watford had to go through the agony of the Play-Offs as the Blades cemented their top two finish. Finishing in fifth position meant that United faced Preston in the Play-Off semi-finals; victory over the two legs — albeit at the cost of a number of suspended players following their sending off — resulted in a final at the Millennium Stadium against Watford. In the event, only one team tuned up at Cardiff and Watford ran out easy 3-0 winners. However, whilst Leeds may now have lost the Premier League parachute payment, the club's liability to a number of erstwhile players has also disappeared and, ironically, the club may well enter the 2006/07 season better placed financially as a result. Provided that Blackwell can retain the bulk of the squad and strengthen it where necessary, United should again be a force in 2006/07 and should undoubtedly feature both in the battle for automatic promotion and for the Play-Offs.

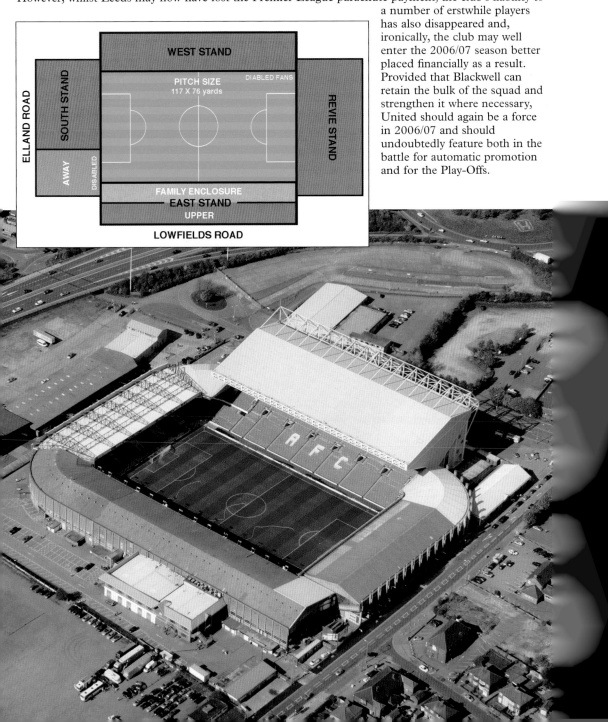

WEST STAND

PITCH SIZE
117 X 76 yards

DIABLED FANS

ELLAND ROAD

SOUTH STAND

AWAY

DISABLED

REVIE STAND

FAMILY ENCLOSURE
EAST STAND
UPPER

LOWFIELDS ROAD

Walkers Stadium, Filbert Way, Leicester, LE2 7FL

Tel No: 0870 040 6000
Advance Tickets Tel No: 0870 499 1884
Fax: 0116 291 1254
Web Site: www.lcfc.premiumtv.co.uk
E-mail: ticket.sales@lcfc.co.uk
League: League Championship
Last Season: 16th (P46; W 13; D 15; L 18; GF 51; GA 59)
Nickname: The Foxes
Brief History: Founded 1884 as Leicester Fosse, changed name to Leicester City in 1919. Former grounds: Fosse Road South, Victoria Road, Belgrave Cycle Track, Mill Lane, Aylstone Road Cricket Ground and Filbert Street (from 1891). The club moved to the new Walkers Stadium for the start of the 2002/03 season. Record attendance (at Filbert Street) 47,298; (at Walkers Stadium) 32,148
(Total) Current Capacity: 32,500

Visiting Supporters' Allocation: 3,000 (all seated) in North East of Ground
Club Colours: Blue shirts, white shorts
Nearest Railway Station: Leicester
Parking (Car): NCP car park
Parking (Coach/Bus): As directed
Police Force and Tel No: Leicester (0116 222 2222)
Disabled Visitors Facilities:
  Wheelchairs: 186 spaces spread through all stands
  Blind: Match commentary via hospital radio
Anticipated Developments: The club moved into the new 32,500-seat Walkers Stadium at the start of the 2002/03 season. Although there are no plans at present, the stadium design allows for the construction of a second tier to the East Stand, taking capacity to 40,000.

KEY

C Club Offices

↑ North direction (approx)

❶ Raw Dykes Road
❷ Eastern Road
❸ A426 Aylestone Road
❹ To Lutterworth
❺ To city centre and railway station (one mile)
❻ Burnmoor Street
❼ River Soar

Above: 699793; *Right:* 699804

Following a 1-0 defeat at fellow strugglers Plymouth Argyle, Craig Levein's 14-month reign at the Walkers Stadium was brought to an end in late January with the Foxes in the League Championship drop zone. Initially appointed as caretaker manager, Rob Kelly was confirmed in the position for the rest of the season following three straight wins that had lifted the Foxes out of the drop zone. Under Kelly's management the team gradually clambered up the League Championship table to finish ultimately in 16th place. Whilst still closer to the drop zone than the Play-Offs, the performances over the second half of the season will encourage the faithful to believe that the 2006/07 season will offer considerably more. Provided that the club can improve its success rate in front of goal, then there is every possibility that a Play-Off place can be achieved but automatic promotion is, perhaps, unlikely.

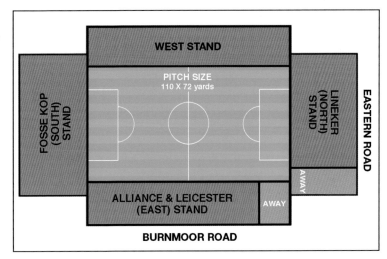

WEST STAND

PITCH SIZE
110 X 72 yards

FOSSE KOP (SOUTH) STAND

LINEKER (NORTH) STAND

EASTERN ROAD

AWAY

ALLIANCE & LEICESTER (EAST) STAND

AWAY

BURNMOOR ROAD

Matchroom Stadium, Brisbane Road, Leyton, London, E10 5NF

Tel No: 020 8926 1111
Advance Tickets Tel No: 020 8926 1010
Fax: 020 8926 1110
Web Site: www.leytonorient.premiumtv.co.uk
E-Mail: info@leytonorient.net
League: League One
Last Season: 3rd (promoted) (P 46; W 22; D 15; L 9; GF 67; GA 51)
Nickname: The O's
Brief History: Founded 1887 as Clapton Orient, from Eagle Cricket Club (formerly Glyn Cricket Club formed in 1881). Changed name to Leyton Orient (1946), Orient (1966), Leyton Orient (1987). Former grounds: Glyn Road, Whittles Athletic Ground, Millfields Road, Lea Bridge Road, Wembley Stadium (2 games), moved to Brisbane Road in 1937. Record attendance 34,345
(Total) Current Capacity: 7,872 (all-seated)
Visiting Supporters' Allocation: 1,000 (all seated) in East Stand/Terrace

Club Colours: Red shirts, red shorts
Nearest Railway Station: Leyton (tube), Leyton Midland Road
Parking (Car): Street parking
Parking (Coach/Bus): As directed by Police
Police Force and Tel No: Metropolitan (020 8556 8855)
Disabled Visitors' Facilities:
　Wheelchairs: Windsor Road
　Blind: Match commentary supplied on request
Anticipated Development(s): The new West Stand, constructed during the 2004/05 season, adds 2,500 to the ground's capacity and also houses club offices and other facilities. This increased the ground's capacity to almost 8,000 from the start of the 2005/06 season. The provision of rental office space in the West Stand is designed to raise income that will ultimately help fund the construction of a new North Stand, construction of which will see Brisbane Road's capacity increase to 10,000.

KEY

C Club Offices
S Club Shop
E Entrance(s) for visiting supporters

↑ North direction (approx)

❶ Buckingham Road
❷ Oliver Road
❸ A112 High Road Leyton
❹ To Leyton Tube Station (¼ mile)
❺ Brisbane Road
❻ Windsor Road
❼ To Leyton Midland Road BR station
❽ South Stand
❾ West Stand
❿ Main (East) Stand

LEYTON ORIENT

Above: 700249; *Right:* 700237

A season of considerable promise at Brisbane Road ultimately came down to the last few minutes of the season when last day drama saw Orient pip Grimsby Town for the final promotion spot from League Two. With Grimsby at home to already promoted Northampton Town and Orient away at relegation threatened Oxford United, it looked until the 90th minute as though Grimsby had survived to take third place; then Northampton equalised and Martin Ling's team scored a winner. The result was delight for the travelling Orient fans, despair for the Oxford United ones — as their team was relegated from the Football League after 44 years — and horror at Grimsby as their fans faced the reality of the Play-Offs. Away from the league, one of the more impressive FA Cup third round matches was Orient's 2-1 victory at Premier League Fulham. It's always a struggle for promoted teams to make the leap upwards, although there are always exceptions as Southend and Swansea proved in League One in 2005/06, but perhaps a season of consolidation is perhaps the best that Orient fans can look forward to.

Sincil Bank, Lincoln, LN5 8LD

Tel No: 0870 899 2005
Advance Tickets Tel No: 0870 899 2005
Fax: 01522 880020
Web Site: www.redimps.premiumtv.co.uk
E-Mail: lcfc@redimps.com
League: League Two
Last Season: 7th (P 46; W 15; D 21; L 10; GF 65; GA 53)
Nickname: The Imps
Brief History: Founded 1884. Former Ground: John O'Gaunts Ground, moved to Sincil Bank in 1895. Founder-members 2nd Division Football League (1892). Relegated from 4th Division in 1987, promoted from GM Vauxhall Conference in 1988. Record attendance 23,196
(Total) Current Capacity: 10,130 (all seated)
Visiting Supporters' Allocation: 2,000 in Co-op Community Stand (part, remainder for Home fans)

Club Colours: Red and white striped shirts, black shorts
Nearest Railway Station: Lincoln Central
Parking (Car): City centre car parks; limited on-street parking
Parking (Coach/Bus): South Common
Police Force and Tel No: Lincolnshire (01522 529911)
Disabled Visitors' Facilities:
  Wheelchairs: The Simons and South (Mundy) Park stands
  Blind: No special facility
Anticipated Development(s): Following the replacement of the seats in the Stacey West Stand, Sincil Bank is once again an all-seater stadium.

LINCOLN CITY

KEY
- **C** Club Offices
- **S** Club Shop
- **E** Entrance(s) for visiting supporters

↑ North direction (approx)

- ❶ A46 High Street
- ❷ Sincil Bank
- ❸ Sausthorpe Street
- ❹ Cross Street
- ❺ Co-op Community Stand (away)
- ❻ A158 South Park Avenue
- ❼ Stacey West Stand
- ❽ Lincoln Central BR Station (¹/₂ mile)
- ❾ Family Stand

Above: 697261; Right: 697523

With the Imps struggling in mid-table, it was announced shortly before the game against Mansfield Town on 2 January (which ended in a 0-0 draw), that manager Keith Alexander and his assistant Gary Simpson had been 'put on leave' and that John Schofield, the youth team coach, would be placed in temporary control of the team. Alexander's suspension lasted less than a week but Simpson left the club 'by mutual agreement'. Earlier in the season, there was a high point with a 5-1 victory over Crewe in the first round of the Carling Cup. The team's performances during the second half of the campaign saw the City gradually climb the League Two table with the result 7th place was secured on the final Saturday of the season and thus, yet again the Play-Offs. How City fans must hate these! In 2004/05 the Imps had been defeated by Southend in the final; in 2005/06, however, the team lost over the two legs of the Semi-Final to local rivals Grimsby Town. After the end of the season, Alexander departed to take over at Peterborough and was replaced by John Schofield as head coach and John Deehan as Director of Football. Thus a further season of League Two football is again on offer at Sincil Bank and it's hard to escape the conclusion that, once again, the Play-Offs may be City's best route to promotion.

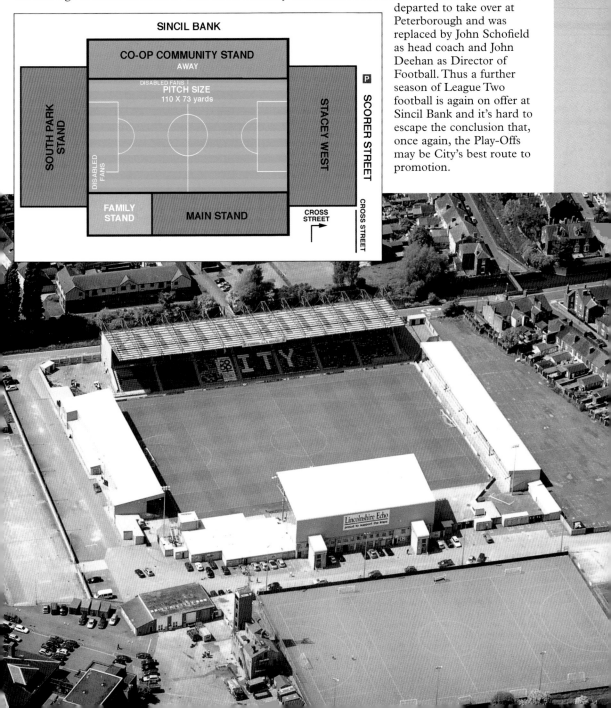

SINCIL BANK

CO-OP COMMUNITY STAND
AWAY

DISABLED FANS
PITCH SIZE
110 X 73 yards

SOUTH PARK STAND

DISABLED FANS

STACEY WEST

P **SCORER STREET**

FAMILY STAND

MAIN STAND

CROSS STREET

CROSS STREET

Anfield Road, Liverpool, L4 0TH

Tel No: 0151 263 2361
Advance Tickets Tel No: 0870 220 2345
Fax: 0151 260 8813
Ticket Enquiries Fax: 0151 261 1416
Web Site: www.liverpoolfc.tv
League: F.A. Premier
Last Season: 3rd (P 38; W 25; D 7; L 6; GF 57; GA 25)
Nickname: The Reds
Brief History: Founded 1892. Anfield Ground formerly Everton F.C. Ground. Joined Football League in 1893. Record attendance 61,905
(Total) Current Capacity: 45,362 (all seated)
Visiting Supporters' Allocation: 1,972 (all seated) in Anfield Road Stand
Club Colours: Red shirts, red shorts
Nearest Railway Station: Kirkdale
Parking (Car): Stanley car park
Parking (Coach/Bus): Priory Road and Pinehurst Avenue

Police Force and Tel No: Merseyside (0151 709 6010)
Disabled Visitors' Facilities:
  Wheelchairs: Kop and Main Stands
  Blind: Commentary available
Anticipated Development(s): In April 2006 the club resubmitted its plans, following the original approval for the construction of the 60,000-seat ground at Stanley Park in 2005, in order to conform to new planning laws. The council again gave planning permission for the £160 million stadium, which, according to latest estimates, could be available by the start of the 2010/11 season. It was recently announced that the Council had taken the first steps in allowing it to be able to dispose of the necessary section of the Park by advertising its availability in order to allow for objections and legal challenges.

KEY

C Club Offices
S Club Shop

↑ North direction (approx)

❶ Car Park
❷ Anfield Road
❸ A5089 Walton Breck Road
❹ Kemlyn Road
❺ Kirkdale BR Station (1 mile)
❻ Utting Avenue
❼ Stanley Park
❽ Spion Kop
❾ Anfield Road Stand

Above: 700015; *Right:* 700030

After the drama of the end of the 2004/05 season, when Liverpool snatched victory from the jaws of defeat in the Champions League final, the new season was always going to be about making a more sustained attempt at the league and, in finishing third (and thereby guaranteeing entry into the Champions League) Rafael Benitez's team just about achieved it. However, a nine-point gap with champions Chelsea shows how big a gulf there is to make up and realistically Liverpool were never really in the hunt for the title in 2005/06. With astute strengthening of the squad in the summer, Liverpool should have the potential to push both Man Utd and Chelsea harder in 2006/07; of the two, United look the weaker and Chelsea, with Michael Ballack amongst a number of high quality players being signed during the summer, stronger. Perhaps second is the best that Reds' fan can look forward to. Apart from the league, Liverpool made a good stab at retaining the Champions League, before being knocked out by Benfica, but were to triumph over West Ham in the FA Cup Final (What is it about Liverpool and Cup Finals? Another 3-3 draw leading to victory on penalties after extra time). With Chelsea's undoubted strength, it is perhaps in the cup competitions that Benitez's team again stands the best chance of adding to the Anfield trophy collection.

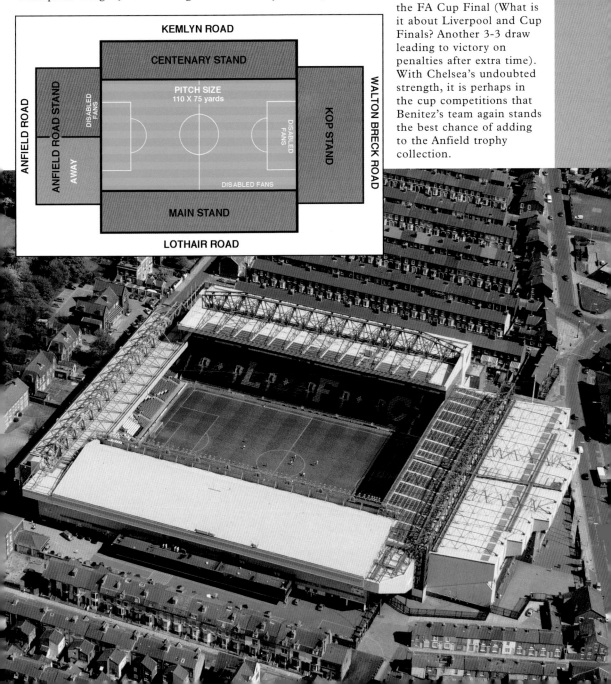

Kenilworth Road Stadium, 1 Maple Road, Luton, LU4 8AW

Tel No: 01582 411622
Advance Tickets Tel No: 01582 416976
Fax: 01582 405070
Web Site: www.lutontown.premiumtv.co.uk
E-Mail: clubsec@lutontown.co.uk
League: League Championship
Last Season: 10th (P 46; W 17; D 10; L 19; GF 66; GA 67)
Nickname: The Hatters
Brief History: Founded 1885 from an amalgamation of Wanderers F.C. and Excelsior F.C. Former Grounds: Dallow Lane & Dunstable Road, moved to Kenilworth Road in 1905. Record attendance 30,069
(Total) Current Capacity: 9,970 (all seated)
Visiting Supporters' Allocation: 2,200
Club Colours: White shirts, black shorts

Nearest Railway Station: Luton
Parking (Car): Street parking
Parking (Coach/Bus): Luton bus station
Police Force and Tel No: Bedfordshire (01582 401212)
Disabled Visitors' Facilities:
  Wheelchairs: Kenilworth Road and Main stands
  Blind: Commentary available
Anticipated Development(s): Towards the end of the 2003/04 season it was announced that the consortium that took the club out of Administration would progress with plans for relocation. The new stadium, to be located close to Junction 10 of the M1, would provide seating for 15,000. The anticipated time-scale was to have the new ground available within three years but nothing is as yet confirmed.

KEY

C Club Offices
E Entrance(s) for visiting supporters
R Refreshment bars for visiting supporters
T Toilets for visiting supporters

↑ North direction (approx)

❶ To M1 Junction 11
❷ Wimborne Road
❸ Kenilworth Road
❹ Oak Road
❺ Dunstable Road
❻ Luton BR Station (1 mile)
❼ Ticket Office

100

Above: 699805; *Right:* 699816

Promoted at the end of the 2004/05 season, the challenge for Mike Newell's team was, like all clubs moving up a division, to consolidate their improved status and, of the three teams promoted at the end of that season, the Hatters were by far the most impressive. For a period it looked as though a Play-Off place was by no means an impossibility although the club wasn't able to sustain this. In finishing 10th, the team has ensured League Championship football at Kenilworth Road again in 2006/07 and laid the foundations for further progress in the new campaign. With the strength of the three relegated teams and the potential weakness of the three teams being promoted from League One, Town should not struggle to retain Championship status during the new season but it's likely that another position mid-table is perhaps the best that can be expected.

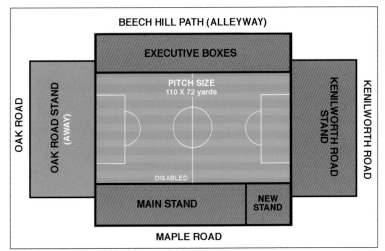

Moss Rose Ground, London Road, Macclesfield, SK11 7SP

Tel No: 01625 264686
Advance Tickets Tel No: 01625 264686
Fax: 01625 264692
Web Site: www.mtfc.premiumtv.co.uk
E-Mail: office@mtfc.co.uk
League: League Two
Last Season: 17th (P 46; W 12; D 18; L 16; GF 60; GA 71)
Nickname: The Silkmen
Brief History: Founded 1874. Previous ground: Rostron Field moved to Moss Rose Ground in 1891. Winners of the Vauxhall Conference in 1994/95 and 1997/97. Admitted to Football League for 1997/98 season. Record attendance 10,041
(Total) Current Capacity: 6,335 (2,599 seated)
Visiting Supporters' Allocation: 1,900 (1,500 in Silkman Terrace; 400 seated in Estate Road Stand)
Club Colours: Royal blue, royal blue shorts
Nearest Railway Station: Macclesfield

Parking (Car): No parking at the ground and the nearest off-street car park is in the town centre (25min walk). There is some on-street parking in the vicinity, but this can get crowded.
Parking (Coach/Bus): As directed
Police Force and Tel No: Cheshire (01625 610000)
Disabled Visitors' Facilities:
  Wheelchairs: 45 places in Estate Road Stand
  Blind: No special facility
Anticipated Development(s): The new Estate Road (Alfred McAlpine) Stand, with its 1,497 seats, was completed towards the end of the 2000/01 season and officially opened on 5 May 2001. This is the first phase of a scheme to redevelop Moss Rose; the next phase will see a seated second tier raised above the existing terrace at the Silkman End. Other recent work has included the provision of permanent toilets at the away end.

KEY
C Club Offices
E Entrance(s) for visiting supporters

↑ North direction (approx)

❶ A523 London Road
❷ To Town Centre and BR station (1.5 miles)
❸ To Leek
❹ Moss Lane
❺ Star Lane
❻ Silkmans Public House (now closed)
❼ Star Lane End
❽ Silkman End (away section)
❾ Estate Road Stand

Above: 697248; *Right:* 697237

MACCLESFIELD TOWN

Having missed out on promotion at the end of the 2004/05 season in the Play-Offs, there was considerable optimism that, under the experienced Brian Horton, the Silkmen would again challenge for at least a Play-Off place during the 2005/06 season. However, for a time it looked as though the team would be moving out of League Two — but in the wrong direction as Town were one of a number of teams that hovered just above the drop zone. In the event, however, the club ultimately finished in a secure — but disappointing — 17th place, five points above relegated Oxford United. Horton remains as manager for the new season and his experience of management at this level should ensure that Town achieve more than in 2005/06 although a top-half finish is perhaps the best that can be hoped for.

STAR LANE

STAR LANE STAND

ESTATE ROAD STAND

AWAY

PITCH SIZE
100 X 66 metres

DISABLED FANS

AWAY SILKMAN END UNCOVERED

UNCOVERED TERRACE

MAIN STAND

LONDON ROAD TERRACE UNCOVERED

A523 LONDON ROAD

The City of Manchester Stadium, Sportcity, Manchester M11 3FF

Tel No: 0870 062 1894
Advance Tickets Tel No: 0870 062 1894
Fax: 0161 438 7999
Web Site: www.mcfc.co.uk
E-mail: mcfc@mcfc.co.uk
League: F.A. Premier
Last Season: 15th (P 38; W 13; D 4; L 21; GF 43; GA 48)
Nickname: The Blues
Brief History: Founded 1880 at West Gorton, changed name to Ardwick (reformed 1887) and to Manchester City in 1894. Former grounds: Clowes Street (1880-81), Kirkmanshulme Cricket Club (1881-82), Queens Road (1882-84), Pink Bank Lane (1884-87), Hyde Road (1887-1923) and Maine Road (from 1923 until 2003). Moved to the City of Manchester Stadium for the start of the 2003/04 season. Founder-members 2nd Division (1892). Record attendance (at Maine Road) 84,569 (record for a Football League Ground); at City of Manchester Stadium 47,304

(Total) Current Capacity: 48,000
Visiting Supporters' Allocation: 3,000 (South Stand); can be increased to 4,500 if required
Club Colours: Sky blue shirts, white shorts
Nearest Railway Station: Manchester Piccadilly
Parking (Car): Ample match day parking available to the north of the stadium, entrance via Alan Turing Way. On-street parking restrictions operate in all areas adjacent to the stadium on matchdays.
Parking (Coach/Bus): Coach parking for visiting supporters is adjacent to turnstiles at Key 103 Stand. For home supporters to the north of the stadium, entrance from Alan Turing Way.
Police Force and Tel No: Greater Manchester (0161 872 5050)
Disabled Visitors' facilities:
  Wheelchairs: 300 disabled seats around ground
  Blind: 14 places alongside helpers in East Stand Level 1. Commentary available via headsets.

MANCHESTER CITY

KEY

↑ North direction (approx)

❶ A662 Ashton New Road
❷ Commonwealth Boulevard
❸ Stadium Way
❹ A6010 Alan Turing Way
❺ North Stand
❻ South (Key 103) Stand
❼ West (Colin Bell) Stand
❽ East Stand
❾ National Squash Centre
❿ Warm-up track
⓫ To Manchester city centre and Piccadilly station (1.5 miles)

Above: 700078; *Right:* 700072

In Stuart Pearce's second full season in charge at City, hopes were high that the club would build upon the success of 2004/05 when a UEFA Cup spot was only missed by a whisker as a result of failing to beat Middlesbrough on the last day. In the event, however, 2005/06 will go down as a season of considerable disappointment with the club ultimately finishing in a poor 15th place. As befits a team managed by 'Psycho', City were reasonably strong defensively and conceded only 48 goals all season in the league but it was up front where the squad struggled, scoring only 43 times. One factor in this was undoubtedly the high profile transfer of Shaun Wright-Phillips to

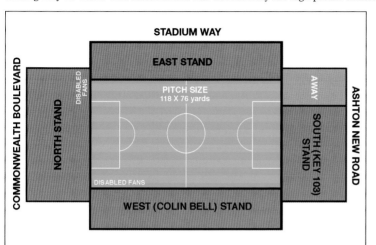

Chelsea as his pace on the wing was an important part of City's tactics. Away from the league, City were to become one of Doncaster Rovers' two Premier league victims during the League One club's impressive run in the Carling cup. At the time of writing, Wright-Phillips, who hasn't had the impact expected with Chelsea, is rumoured to be making a return to City probably on loan; if that's the case then Pearce may be able to make City a more successful outfit in 2006/07. A top half finish should certainly be possible although it's looking rather crowded at the top for a UEFA Cup spot.

Old Trafford, Sir Matt Busby Way, Manchester, M16 0RA

Tel No: 0161 868 8000
Advance Tickets Tel No: 0870 442 1999
Fax: 0161 868 8804
Web Site: www.manutd.com
E-mail: enquiries@manutd.co.uk
League: F.A. Premier
Last Season: 2nd (P 38; W 25; D 8; L 5; GF 72; GA 34)
Nickname: The Red Devils
Brief History: Founded in 1878 as 'Newton Heath L&Y', later Newton Heath, changed to Manchester United in 1902. Former Grounds: North Road, Monsall & Bank Street, Clayton, moved to Old Trafford in 1910 (used Manchester City F.C. Ground 1941-49). Founder-members Second Division (1892). Record attendance 76,962
(Total) Current Capacity: 76,000 (all seated)
Visiting Supporters' Allocation: Approx. 3,000 in corner of South and East Stands

Club Colours: Red shirts, white shorts
Nearest Railway Station: At Ground
Parking (Car): Lancashire Cricket Ground and White City
Parking (Coach/Bus): As directed by Police
Police Force and Tel No: Greater Manchester (0161 872 5050)
Disabled Visitors' Facilities:
  Wheelchairs: South East Stand
  Blind: Commentary available
Anticipated Development(s): The work on the £45 million project construct infills at the north-east and north-west corners of the ground has now been completed and takes Old Trafford's capacity to 76,000, making it by some margin the largest league ground in Britain. Any future development of the ground will involve the Main (South) stand although work here is complicated by the proximity of the building to the adjacent railway line.

KEY
C Club Offices

↑ North direction (approx)

❶ To A5081 Trafford Park Road to M63 Junction 4 (5 miles)
❷ A56 Chester Road
❸ Bridgewater Canal
❹ To Old Trafford Cricket Ground
❺ To Parking and Warwick Road BR Station
❻ Sir Matt Busby Way
❼ North Stand
❽ South Stand
❾ West Stand
❿ East Stand

Above: 700123; *Right:* 700124

Although the already extensive trophy cabinet at Old Trafford was further extended in 2005/06 — courtesy of the Carling Cup victory over Wigan Athletic — in many respects the past season was not one of the greatest for United. Although the title race was not settled until later than many had anticipated and the number of points separating United from Chelsea was reduced from the previous year, the title always looked to be Chelsea's to lose with the real battle to be who came second. More pertinently, however, failure in the Champions League group stages resulted in an early exit from European competition, with not even a UEFA Cup spot to compensate, and elsewhere ructions with senior members of the squad led to the departure of Roy Keane. If a single moment perhaps encapsulated United's season, it was the injury to Wayne Rooney in the match against Chelsea that confirmed the Londoners as title winners and scuppered Rooney's hopes of untroubled passage to the World Cup. Finishing second ensures Sir Alex Ferguson's team automatic entry to the Champions League group stages and it perhaps in the cup competitions that Ferguson's best hopes of adding to his large collection of winners medals lie (although probably not the Champions League). It's hard to escape the conclusion that United will again make a strong bid for second in the Premier League but that the title itself may well be beyond them.

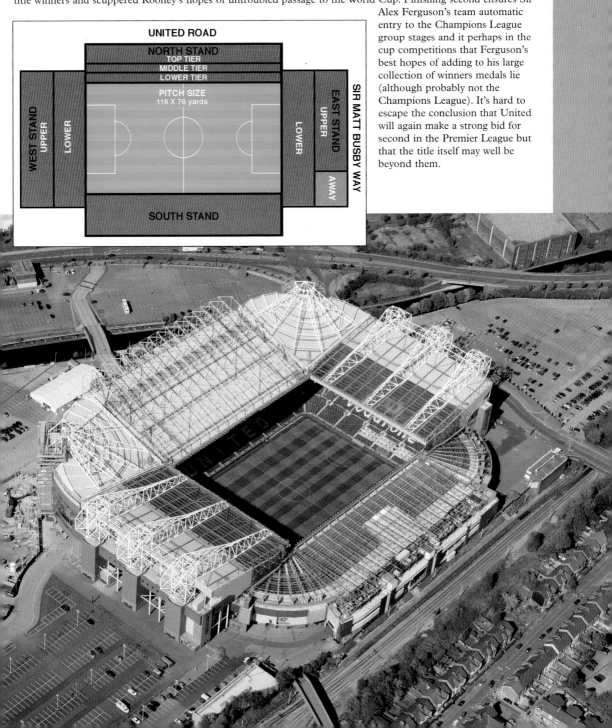

UNITED ROAD

NORTH STAND
TOP TIER
MIDDLE TIER
LOWER TIER

PITCH SIZE
116 X 76 yards

WEST STAND
UPPER
LOWER

EAST STAND
UPPER
LOWER

AWAY

SIR MATT BUSBY WAY

SOUTH STAND

Field Mill Stadium, Quarry Lane, Mansfield, Notts, NG18 5DA

Tel No: 0870 756 3160
Advance Tickets Tel No: 0870 756 3160
Fax: 01623 482495
Web Site: www.mansfieldtown.premiumtv.co.uk
E-mail: stags@stags.plus.com
League: League Two
Last Season: 16th (P46; W 13; D 15; L 18; GF 59; GA 66)
Nickname: The Stags
Brief History: Founded 1910 as Mansfield Wesleyans Boys Brigade, changed to Mansfield Town in 1914. Former Grounds: Pelham Street, Newgate Lane and The Prairie, moved to Field Mill in 1919. Record attendance 24,467
(Total) Current Capacity: 9,990 (all seated)
Visiting Supporters' Allocation: 1,800 (all seated) in North Stand

Club Colours: Amber with blue trim shirts, Blue shorts with amber trim
Nearest Railway Station: Mansfield
Parking (Car): Car park at Ground
Parking (Coach/Bus): Car park at Ground
Police Force and Tel No: Nottinghamshire (01623 420999)
Disabled Visitors' Facilities:
  Wheelchairs: Facilities provided in North, West and South stands
  Blind: No special facility
Anticipated Development(s): Work on the Main Stand and on the North and Quarry Lane ends was completed in early 2001, leaving the Bishop Street Stand as the only unreconstructed part of Field Mill. Plans exist for this to be rebuilt as a 2,800-seat structure but the time scale is unconfirmed.

MANSFIELD TOWN

KEY

E Entrance(s) for visiting supporters

↑ North direction (approx)

❶ Car Park(s)
❷ Quarry Lane
❸ A60 Nottingham Road to M1 Junction 27
❹ Portland Street
❺ To A38 and M1 Junction 28
❻ To Town Centre
❼ Mansfield railway station
❽ North Stand (away)
❾ Quarry Lane End (South Stand)
❿ Bishop Street Stand
⓫ Main (West) Stand

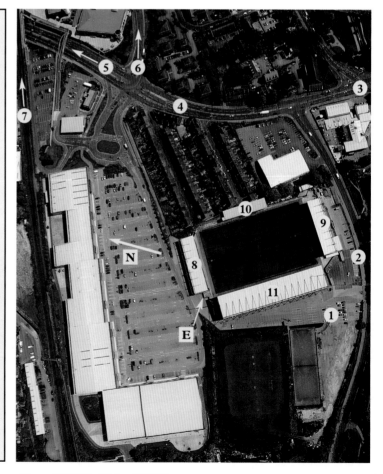

Above: 698870; *Right:* 698878

In mid-September, following a 2-0 reverse away at high-flying Rochdale which left the Stags in 22nd place, Carlton Palmer resigned as manager with Peter Shirtliff taking over as caretaker. Under Shirtliff, the club's fortunes improved and the team gradually pulled away from the drop-zone, ultimately finishing in 16th place some five points above relegated Oxford despite a last day thrashing by Play-Off chasing Cheltenham Town at Field Mill.

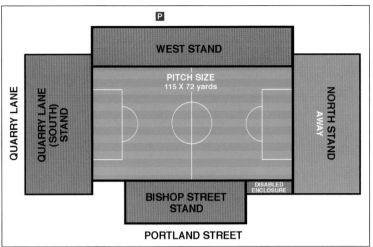

A 5-0 drubbing was not what the fans were looking for in the final game of the season and the score certainly affected the club's Goals Against total! Two highpoints of the season were victory, after penalties, over Championship outfit Stoke City in the first round of the Carling Cup and a 1-0 defeat over Southampton in the second round (in the first game after Palmer's departure). Looking to the new season, Shirtliff will be looking to bring in new players to strengthen the squad although another season in mid-table looks the most likely scenario in this part of Nottinghamshire.

Riverside Stadium, Middlesbrough, Cleveland TS3 6RS

Tel No: 0870 421 1986
Advance Tickets Tel No: 0870 421 1986
Fax: 01642 877840
Web Site: www.mfc.co.uk
E-mail: media.dept@mfc.co.uk
League: F.A. Premier
Last Season: 14th (P 38; W 12; D 9; L 17; GF 48; GA 58)
Nickname: Boro
Brief History: Founded 1876. Former Grounds: Archery Ground (Albert Park), Breckon Hill Road, Linthorpe Road, moved to Ayresome Park in 1903, and to current ground in Summer 1995. F.A. Amateur Cup winners 1894 and 1897 (joined Football League in 1899). Record attendance (Ayresome Park) 53,596, (Riverside Stadium) 35,000
(Total) Current Capacity: 35,100 (all seated)
Visiting Supporters' Allocation: 3,450 (in the South Stand)

Club Colours: Red shirts, red shorts
Nearest Railway Station: Middlesbrough
Parking (Car): All parking at stadium is for permit holders
Parking (Coach/Bus): As directed
Police Force and Tel No: Cleveland (01642 248184)
Disabled Visitors' Facilities:
  Wheelchairs: More than 170 places available for disabled fans
  Blind: Commentary available
Anticipated Development(s): There remain long term plans for the ground's capacity to be increased to 42,000 through the construction of extra tiers on the North, South and East stands, although there is no confirmed timetable for this work at the current time.

MIDDLESBROUGH

KEY
C Club Offices
S Club Shop

⬆ North direction (approx)

❶ Cargo Fleet Road
❷ To Middlesbrough railway station
❸ To Middlesbrough town centre
❹ Middlesbrough Docks
❺ Shepherdson Way to A66
❻ South Stand
❼ Car parks

Above: 697413; *Right:* 697417

It's doubtful if the Boro' faithful had ever had such a season of ups and downs. On the one hand, defeats 7-0 away at Arsenal and 4-0 at home to Villa — the latter score resulting in a disgusted fan throwing his season ticket at Steve McLaren — as well as struggling to defeat non-league Tamworth in the FA Cup hinted at problems on the field; on the other hand dramatic last minute winners against Basle and Steua Bucharest in the UEFA Cup resulted in the team reaching a European cup final for the first time in its history. Facing Seville at Eindhoven was, however, a game too far, and Boro' never really showed the team's potential in ultimately losing 4-0 (although it might have been very different if the referee had given a penalty mid-way through the second half when Boro' were only 1-0 down). One can't help feeling, though, that the end of the 2005/06 season marks an end of an era at the Riverside Stadium; Steve McLaren is moving on to take over as England manager and many of the more seasoned players have perhaps played their last game for the club. The new manager, Gareth Southgate (a tyro manager if ever there was one whose appointment, without the relevant qualifications has not been universally approved and represents a considerable gamble by chairman Steve Gibson), will inherit a team bursting with young players that have been forced through injuries to gain experience beyond their years. How well the club performs in the 2006/07 season may well depend on how good — or bad — the season starts; Boro' seems to be a team that thrives best when confidence is high — a poor start could make the season one of a struggle.

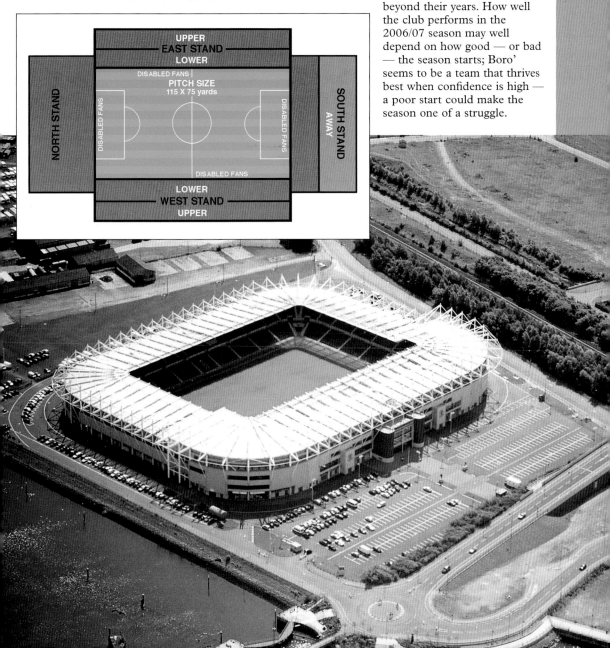

New Den, Bolina Road, London, SE16 3LN

Tel No: 020 7232 1222
Advance Tickets Tel No: 020 7231 9999
Fax: 020 7231 3663
Web Site: www.millwallfc.premiumtv.co.uk
E-mail: questions@millwallplc.com
League: League One
Last Season: 23rd (relegated) (P 46; W 8; D 16; L 22; GF 35; GA 62)
Nickname: The Lions
Brief History: Founded 1885 as Millwall Rovers, changed name to Millwall Athletic (1889) and Millwall (1925). Former Grounds: Glengall Road, East Ferry Road (2 separate Grounds), North Greenwich Ground and The Den – Cold Blow Lane – moved to New Den 1993/94 season. Founder-members Third Division (1920). Record attendance (at The Den) 48,672 (at New Den) 20,093

(Total) Current Capacity: 20,150 (all seated)
Visiting Supporters' Allocation: 4,382 in North Stand
Club Colours: Blue shirts, white shorts
Nearest Railway Station: South Bermondsey or Surrey Docks (Tube)
Parking (Car): Juno Way car parking (8 mins walk)
Parking (Coach/Bus): At Ground
Police Force and Tel No: Metropolitan (0207 679 9217)
Disabled Visitors' Facilities:
Wheelchairs: 200 spaces in West Stand Lower Tier
Blind: Commentary available

KEY
C Club Offices
S Club Shop
E Entrance(s) for visiting supporters

↑ North direction (approx)

❶ Bolina Road
❷ To South Bermondsey station
❸ Footpath to station for away fans
❹ Zampa Road
❺ Stockholm Road
❻ North Stand (away)

Above: 697379; *Right:* 697384

The first managerial casualty of the 2005/06 season occurred before the start of the campaign when Millwall dismissed Steve Claridge after only 36 days in charge. Colin Lee, who had been brought in a few days earlier as coach, immediately stepped up to take full control of the team. Lee survived as manager until mid-December when, with the club rooted to the bottom of the Championship, new chairman Peter de Savary announced that Lee would become the club's Director of Football and 33-year-old David Tuttle would take over as manager until the end of the season. However, Tuttle wasn't able to arrest the club's decline and relegation was confirmed as a result of Sheffield Wednesday's victory over fellow strugglers. Tuttle departed before the end of the season, with Tony Burns and Alan McLeary taking over for the final two games of the campaign. New manager Nigel Spackman, back in management after a five-year gap, will have a struggle in League One; although, as a relegated team, the Lions should have a reasonable chance of making the Play-Offs at worst, there are a number of highly ambitious teams in League One — such as Forest and Bristol City — with the result that it could be a difficult division to climb out of in 2006/07.

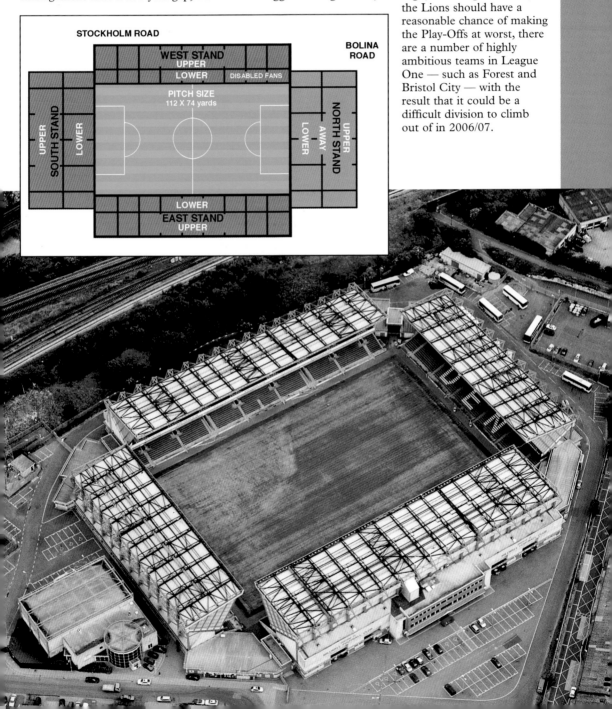

STOCKHOLM ROAD

BOLINA ROAD

WEST STAND
UPPER
LOWER   DISABLED FANS

PITCH SIZE
112 X 74 yards

UPPER
SOUTH STAND

LOWER

UPPER
NORTH STAND
AWAY
LOWER

LOWER
EAST STAND
UPPER

National Hockey Stadium, Silbury Boulevard, Milton Keynes, MK9 1FA

Tel No: 01908 607090
Advance Tickets Tel No: 01908 609000
Fax: 01908 209449
National Hockey Stadium: 01908 246800
Web Site: www.mkdons.premiumtv.co.uk
E-Mail: info@mkdons.com
League: League Two
Last Season: 22nd (relegated) (P46; W 12; D 14; L 20; GF 45; GA 66)
Nickname: The Dons
Brief History: Founded 1889 at Wimbledon Old Centrals, changed name to Wimbledon in 1905 and to Milton Keynes Dons in 2004. Former grounds: Wimbledon Common, Pepy's Road, Grand Drive, Merton Hall Road, Malden Wanderers Cricket Ground, Plough Lane and moved to Selhurst Park in 1991. Probable move to National Hockey Stadium 2002. Elected to Football League in 1977. Record attendance (Plough Lane) 18,000; (Selhurst Park) 30,115; (National Hockey Stadium) 8,118

(Total) Current Capacity: 9,000 (all seated)
Visiting Supporters' Allocation: 2,300 (West Stand) plus 1,000 on North Stand if required
Club Colours: White shirts, White shorts
Nearest Railway Station: Milton Keynes Central
Parking (Car): At ground
Parking (Coach/Bus): As directed
Police Force and Tel No: Thames Valley Police (01865 846000)
Disabled Visitors' Facilities:
  Wheelchairs: 48 spaces around the ground
  Blind: No special facility at present
Anticipated Development(s): Work started on the construction of the club's new 30,000-seat capacity stadium in mid-February 2005. Although the ground will be completed during the course of the 2006/07 season, the club will not move in until the start of the 2007/08 season.

KEY

↑ North direction (approx)

❶ West Stand (away)
❷ To Milton Keynes Central station
❸ Grafton Gate
❹ A509 Portway
❺ A509 Portway to A5 junction
❻ Silbury Boulevard
❼ To town centre

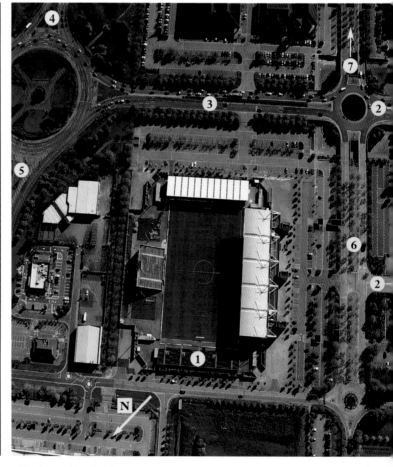

Above: 698885; *Right:* 698894

Following their survival in League One at the end of the 2004/05 season, many anticipated that the Dons would struggle in their final full season at the Nation Hockey Stadium if the club was not to start its life in new ground in League Two and, in this, the pundits were not to be disappointed. However, despite having looked dead and buried for much of the campaign, a late upturn in form saw the Dons come within an ace of League survival, with results on the last day determining the club's fate. The final crunch match was at fellow struggler Rotherham where, effectively, the team that lost was relegated. In the event, a 0-0 draw, combined with results elsewhere, was enough to secure the Millers' survival and relegation to League Two for the Dons. Within days of the end of the season manager Danny Wilson, in place since 2004, was sacked and new manager Martin Allen will have a major task in making the club a force in League Two.

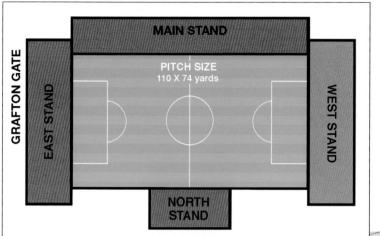

St. James' Park, Newcastle-upon-Tyne, NE1 4ST

Tel No: 0191 201 8400
Advance Tickets Tel No: 0191 261 1571
Fax: 0191 201 8600
Web Site: www.nufc.premiumtv.co.uk
E-mail: custserv@nufc.co.uk
League: F.A. Premier
Last Season: 7th (P 38; W 17; D 7; L 14; GF 47; GA 42)
Nickname: The Magpies
Brief History: Founded in 1882 as Newcastle East End, changed to Newcastle United in 1892. Former Grounds: Chillingham Road, moved to St. James' Park (former home of defunct Newcastle West End) in 1892. Record attendance 68,386
(Total) Current Capacity: 52,316 (all seated)
Visiting Supporters' Allocation: 3,000 in North West Stand
Club Colours: Black and white striped shirts, black shorts

Nearest Railway Station: Newcastle Central
Parking (Car): Leazes car park and street parking
Parking (Coach/Bus): Leazes car park
Police Force and Tel No: Northumbria (0191 232 3451)
Disabled Visitors' Facilities:
  Wheelchairs: 103 spaces available
  Blind: Commentary available
Anticipated Development(s): With work now completed on both the enlarged Millburn and Sir John Hall stands, the capacity at St James' Park is now about 52,000. Further redevelopment at the ground is, however, problematic given the lie of the land on the north side, and the club has no immediate plans for further work once the current programme is completed.

NEWCASTLE UNITED

KEY
C Club Offices
S Club Shop

↑ North direction (approx)

❶ St. James's Park
❷ Strawberry Place
❸ Gallowgate
❹ Away Section
❺ To Newcastle Central BR Station (1/2 mile) & A6127(M)
❻ Car Park
❼ Barrack Road (A189)
❽ To A1 and North
❾ Corporation Street
❿ Gallowgate End
⓫ Metro Station
⓬ Sir John Hall Stand
⓭ Millburn Stand
⓮ East Stand

Above: 700356; *Right:* 700351

After much speculation and with the Magpies languishing in 15th place in the Premiership after a 3-0 defeat at Manchester City, Graeme Souness was sacked as manager in early February after some 16 months in the St James's Park hot-seat. Despite the high-profile arrival of Michael Owen, who soon joined the club's injury list, and other players Souness struggled to bring success to the team with only 36 victories during his 83 matches in charge. Following his departure, Glenn Roeder took over as caretaker manager with Alan Shearer as his assistant. At the time, it was stated that Roeder's appointment would be only to the end of the season as he lacked the relevant professional qualifications to take the role on a full-time basis. Under Roeder's leadership, the club's fortunes improved immeasurably and it came as no surprise that the club sought dispensation to allow Roeder to continue in his role for the new season. Finishing in 7th place was a distinct improvement on what had looked likely earlier in the season and, provided that the team can avoid the serious injuries that

deprived them of Owen and others for much of the season and can find a strong replacement for the retiring Alan Shearer, there must be every hope that the Magpies can again challenge for at least a UEFA Cup spot. The reality is, however, that United's best chance for silverware may well come through one of the cup competitions.

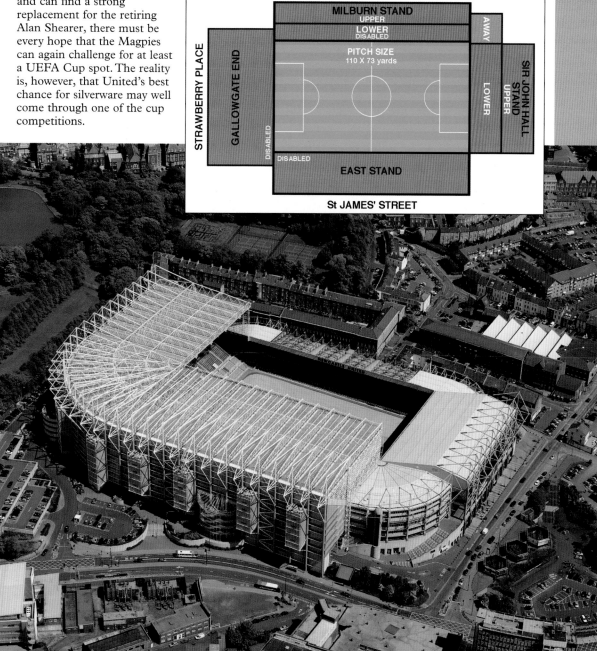

Sixfields Stadium, Northampton, NN5 5QA

Tel No: 0870 822 1897
Advance Tickets Tel No: 0870 822 1897
Fax: 01604 751613
Web Site: www.ntfc.premiumtv.co.uk
E-Mail: normanhowells@ntfc.tv
League: League Two
Last Season: 2nd (promoted) (P 46; W 22; D 17; L 7; GF 63; GA 37)
Nickname: The Cobblers
Brief History: Founded 1897. Former, County, Ground was part of Northamptonshire County Cricket Ground. Moved to Sixfields Stadium during early 1994/95 season. Record attendance 24,523 (at County Ground); 7,557 (at Sixfields)
(Total) Current Capacity: 7,653 (all seated)
Visiting Supporters' Allocation: 850 (in South Stand; can be increased to 1,150 if necessary)

Club Colours: Claret with white sleeved shirts, white shorts
Nearest Railway Station: Northampton
Parking (Car): Adjacent to Ground
Parking (Coach/Bus): Adjacent to Ground
Police Force and Tel No: Northants (01604 700700)
Disabled Visitors' Facilities:
  Wheelchairs: Available on all four sides
  Blind: Available
Anticipated Development(s): The club has plans to increase the capacity of the Sixfields stadium to c16,000 all-seated although there is no timescale for this work.

KEY

C Club Offices
S Club Shop
E Entrance(s) for visiting supporters
R Refreshment bars for visiting supporters
T Toilets for visiting supporters

↑ North direction (approx)

❶ South Stand (away)
❷ Athletics Stand
❸ Upton Way
❹ Car parks
❺ A45 towards A43 (Towcester and A5)
❻ To Weedon Road
❼ To Town Centre and station
❽ A45 to M1 (Jct 16)

Above: 699879; Right: 699819

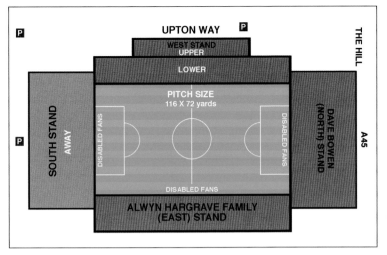

UPTON WAY

P · P

WEST STAND
UPPER

LOWER

PITCH SIZE
116 X 72 yards

SOUTH STAND

AWAY

DISABLED FANS

DISABLED FANS

DAVE BOWEN
(NORTH) STAND

THE HILL

A45

P

DISABLED FANS

ALWYN HARGRAVE FAMILY
(EAST) STAND

A season that seemed to have been hugely successful for the Cobblers ultimately ended with an anti-climax as it was announced after the end of the campaign that Colin Calderwood, who had been in charge at Sixfields for three years, had left to take over at Nottingham Forest. Under Calderwood, Town had made impressive progress during the 2005/06 season and it was no great surprise when the team ensured automatic promotion to League One with a 3-1 victory over struggling Oxford United at the Kassam Stadium. Away from the league, the team also secured an impressive 3-0 victory over Championship side QPR in the first round of the Carling Cup. With a number of the backroom staff following Calderwood to the City ground, Town's new manager — the experienced John Gorman — will have his work cut out to ensure that the team does not make a swift return to the Football League's basement division. In the circumstances, perhaps a season of consolidation is the best that Cobblers' fans can look forward to.

Carrow Road, Norwich, NR1 1JE

Tel No: 01603 760760
Advance Tickets Tel No: 0870 444 1902
Fax: 01603 613886
Web Site: www.canaries.premiumtv.co.uk
E-Mail: reception@ncfc-canaries.co.uk
League: League Championship
Last Season: 9th (P46; W 18; D 8; L 20; GF 56; GA 64)
Nickname: The Canaries
Brief History: Founded 1902. Former grounds: Newmarket Road and the Nest, Rosary Road; moved to Carrow Road in 1935. Founder-members 3rd Division (1920). Record attendance 43,984
(Total) Current Capacity: 26,034
Visiting Supporters' Allocation: 2,500 maximum in South Stand
Club Colours: Yellow with green side panel shirts, green shorts
Nearest Railway Station: Norwich

Parking (Car): City centre car parks
Parking (Coach/Bus): Lower Clarence Road
Police Force and Tel No: Norfolk (01603 768769)
Disabled Visitors' Facilities:
Wheelchairs: New facility in corner infill stand
Blind: Commentary available
Anticipated Development(s): The £3 million corner infill between the new Jarrold (South) Stand and the River End was opened in two stages in early 2005. The upper tier provides seats for 850 and the lower for 660. There is also a new disabled area located between the two tiers. This work takes Carrow Road's capacity to 26,000. As part of the plans for the Jarrold Stand, the pitch was relocated one metre away from the City Stand; this will facilitate the construction of a second tier on the City Stand in the future if required.

KEY

C Club Offices
S Club Shop

↑ North direction (approx)

❶ Carrow Road
❷ A47 King Street
❸ River Wensum
❹ Riverside
❺ Car Park
❻ Norwich BR Station
❼ South (Jarrold) Stand
❽ Geoffrey Watling (City) Stand
❾ Barclay End Stand
❿ The Norwich & Peterborough (River End) Stand

Above: 698898; *Right:* 698903

Relegated from the Premier League at the end of the 2004/05 season, most pundits anticipated that Nigel Worthington's team would be one of the favourites to make an automatic return to the top flight of English football, particularly as the majority of the squad had remained. Critically, perhaps, given the team's goal shyness, Dean Ashton departed for West Ham United. However, at the start of the season it looked as though the team would be battling to remain in the division at the wrong end rather than escaping it from the top as the Canaries seemed rooted to the bottom half of the table; an improvement in results during the second half of the campaign ultimately saw the team reach a flattering 9th position but this was some 28 points off the promotion places and even 13 of the Play-Offs. If City are to make further progress in 2006/07 then there is an undoubted need to strengthen the strike force as well as improve the defence (relegated Millwall, for example, conceded fewer goals than City). With judicious strengthening of the squad, Worthington's team should feature in the battle for a top-six position.

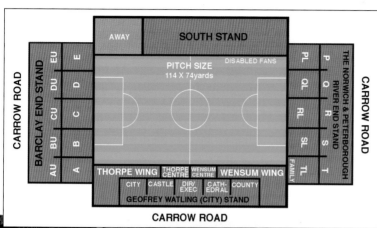

City Ground, Nottingham, NG2 5FJ

Tel No: 0115 982 4444
Advance Tickets Tel No: 0871 226 1980
Fax: 0115 982 4455
Web Site: www.nottinghamforest.premiumtv.co.uk
E-Mail: enquiries@nottinghamforest.co.uk
League: League One
Last Season: 7th (P46; W 19; D 12; L 15; GF 67; GA 52)
Nickname: The Reds
Brief History: Founded 1865 as Forest Football Club, changed name to Nottingham Forest (c1879). Former Grounds: Forest Recreation Ground, Meadow Cricket Ground, Trent Bridge (Cricket Ground), Parkside, Gregory Ground and Town Ground, moved to City Ground in 1898. Founder-members of Second Division (1892). Record attendance 49,945

(Total) Current Capacity: 30,602 (all seated)
Visiting Supporters' Allocation: Approx 4,750
Club Colours: Red shirts, white shorts
Nearest Railway Station: Nottingham
Parking (Car): East car park and street parking
Parking (Coach/Bus): East car park
Police Force and Tel No: Nottinghamshire (0115 948 1888)
Disabled Visitors' Facilities:
   Wheelchairs: Front of Brian Clough Stand
   Blind: No special facility
Anticipated Development(s): The club has long-term plans for the redevelopment of the Main Stand, with a view to increasing the ground's capacity to 40,000, but nothing will happen until the club reclaims a position in the Premiership.

NOTTINGHAM FOREST

KEY

C Club Offices
S Club Shop
E Entrance(s) for visiting supporters

↑ North direction (approx)

❶ Radcliffe Road
❷ Lady Bay Bridge Road
❸ Trent Bridge
❹ Trent Bridge Cricket Ground
❺ Bridgford Stand
❻ River Trent
❼ Nottingham Midland BR Station (1/2 mile)

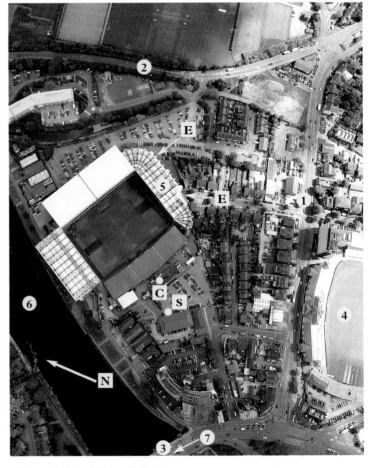

Above: 698938; Right: 698930

Relegated at the end of 2004/05, much was expected from Forest in their first season at League One level for more than 50 years. However, a mediocre campaign saw the team languishing in mid-table by February when, after a 3-0 defeat at Oldham, Gary Megson departed from the City Ground after 13 months in charge. Ian McParland and Frank Barlow were appointed joint caretaker managers although neither was willing to be considered for the post on a permanent basis. As with Bristol City, the change of management brought an improvement in form on the field and a rapid rise up the League One table. Towards the end of the campaign, Forest were within grasping distance of grabbling the last of the Play-Off places; unfortunately, however, last day results, with Forest drawing 1-1 at Bradford City, resulted in the club finishing below the all-important sixth position and thus League One fare will again be on offer at the City Ground in 2006/07. New boss Colin Calderwood, who guided Northampton Town to League One at the end of the 2005/06 season, will take a club better placed than Messrs McParland and Barlow did in the spring; Forest ought to be one of the challengers for automatic promotion.

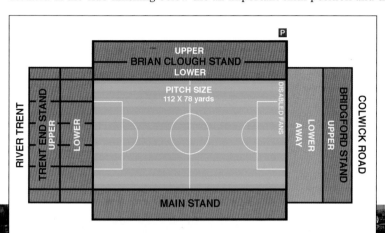

Meadow Lane, Nottingham, NG2 3HJ

Tel No: 0115 952 9000
Advance Tickets Tel No: 0115 955 7204
Fax: 0115 955 3994
Web Site: www.nottscountyfc.premiumtv.co.uk
E-Mail: info@nottscountyfc.co.uk
League: League Two
Last Season: 21st (P46; W 12; D 16; L 18; GF 48; GA 63)
Nickname: The Magpies
Brief History: Founded 1862 (oldest club in Football League) as Nottingham, changed to Notts County in c1882. Former Grounds: Notts Cricket Ground (Beeston), Castle Cricket Ground, Trent Bridge Cricket Ground, moved to Meadow Lane in 1910. Founder-members Football League (1888). Record attendance 47,310

(Total) Current Capacity: 20,700 (seated)
Visiting Supporters' Allocation: 5,438 (seated)
Club Colours: Black and white striped shirts, black shorts
Nearest Railway Station: Nottingham Midland
Parking (Car): Mainly street parking
Parking (Coach/Bus): Cattle market
Police Force and Tel No: Nottingham (0115 948 1888)
Disabled Visitors' Facilities:
  Wheelchairs: Meadow Lane/Jimmy Sirrel/Derek Pavis Stands
  Blind: No special facility

NOTTS COUNTY

KEY

E Entrance(s) for visiting supporters

R Refreshment bars for visiting supporters

T Toilets for visiting supporters

↑ North direction (approx)

❶ A6011 Meadow Lane
❷ County Road
❸ A60 London Road
❹ River Trent
❺ Nottingham Midland BR Station (1/2 mile)
❻ Jimmy Sirrel Stand
❼ Kop Stand (away)
❽ Derek Pavis Stand
❾ Family (Meadow Lane) Stand

Above: 698926; *Right:* 698913

For much of the season it looked as though the Football League was going to have to find a new 'oldest club' as County hovered dangerously close to the League Two drop zone and thus relegation to the Conference. Indeed, it was not until the final Saturday of the season that the Magpies' League status was preserved. One of a number of teams that could have joined Rushden & Diamonds in relegation, County, however, survived courtesy of a 2-2 draw at Meadow Lane against fellow strugglers Bury. This left County two places and three points above the drop zone and, shortly after the end of the season, it was confirmed that Icelandic boss Gudjon Thordarsson was leaving the club after only a season in charge. He was replaced by Steve Thompson; however, as last year, it's hard to escape the conclusion that another battle against relegation beckons, particularly if the team continues to struggle to score goals.

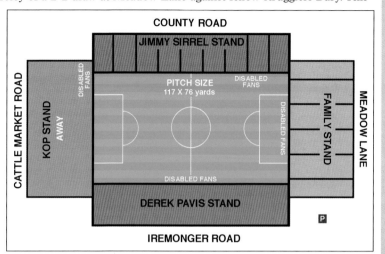

COUNTY ROAD

JIMMY SIRREL STAND

CATTLE MARKET ROAD

KOP STAND
AWAY

DISABLED FANS

PITCH SIZE
117 X 76 yards

DISABLED FANS

DISABLED FANS

DISABLED FANS

FAMILY STAND

MEADOW LANE

DEREK PAVIS STAND

P

IREMONGER ROAD

Boundary Park, Oldham, OL1 2PA

Tel No: 0871 226 2235
Advance Tickets Tel No: 0871 226 2235
Fax: 0871 226 1715
Web Site: www.oldhamathletic.premiumtv.co.uk
E-Mail: enquiries@oldhamathletic.co.uk
League: League One
Last Season: 10th (P 46; W 18; D 11; L 17; GF 58; GA 60)
Nickname: The Latics
Brief History: Founded 1897 as Pine Villa, changed name to Oldham Athletic in 1899. Former Grounds: Berry's Field, Pine Mill, Athletic Ground (later named Boundary Park), Hudson Fold, moved to Boundary Park in 1906. Record attendance 47,671
(Total) Current Capacity: 13,624 (all seated)
Visiting Supporters' Allocation: 1,800 minimum, 4,600 maximum
Club Colours: Blue shirts, blue shorts
Nearest Railway Station: Oldham Werneth
Parking (Car): Lookers Stand car park

Parking (Coach/Bus): At Ground
Other Clubs Sharing Ground: Oldham Roughyeads RLFC
Police Force and Tel No: Greater Manchester (0161 624 0444)
Disabled Visitors' Facilities:
  Wheelchairs: Rochdale Road and Seton Stands
  Blind: No special facility
Anticipated Development(s): Although the club originally had plans to relocate, it was announced in February that it was going to seek Planning Permission late in 2006 for the redevelopment of Boundary Park. The proposed £80 million plan would see three sides of the ground rebuilt with the intention of obtaining a 16,000 capacity. The redevelopment would also include a hotel, fitness club and offices. Other than the club awaits Planning Permission, there is no time scale for the work.

KEY

C Club Offices
E Entrance(s) for visiting supporters

⬆ North direction (approx)

❶ A663 Broadway
❷ Furtherwood Road
❸ Chadderton Way
❹ To A627(M) and M62
❺ To Oldham Werneth BR Station (1½ miles)
❻ Car Park
❼ Rochdale Road Stand (away)
❽ SSL Stand
❾ Lookers Stand
❿ Pukka Pies Stand

OLDHAM ATHLETIC

Above: 697199; Right: 697195

Having just escaped relegation at the end of the 2004/05 season on the last day Ronnie Moore's Oldham outfit proved to be made of sterner stuff in 2005/06. Although a Play-Off berth seemed a possibility at one stage, the club ultimately finished in mid-table — a considerable improvement over the previous season but clearly not good enough for the club. In early June it was announced that Moore, who had been in charge since March 2005, was being dismissed and that he would be replaced by John Sheridan. In 2005/06 League One proved to be very tight with only 21 points separating the Play-Offs from the relegation zone and it's hard to escape the conclusion that the new season will be equally tight. Oldham should be one of the teams again challenging for the former, but a poor start and a few dropped points could equally see the latter.

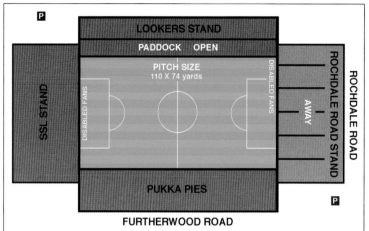

PETERBOROUGH UNITED

London Road, Peterborough, Cambs, PE2 8AL

Tel No: 01733 563947
Advance Tickets Tel No: 01753 563947
Fax: 01733 344140
Web Site: www.theposh.premiumtv.co.uk
E-Mail: info@theposh.com
League: League Two
Last Season: 9th (P46; W 17; D 11; L 18; GF 57; GA 49)
Nickname: Posh
Brief History: Founded in 1934 (no connection with former 'Peterborough and Fletton United' FC). Elected to Football League in 1960. Record attendance 30,096
(Total) Current Capacity: 15,314 (7,669 seated)
Visiting Supporters' Allocation: 4,758 (756 seated)

Club Colours: Blue shirts, white shorts
Nearest Railway Station: Peterborough
Parking (Car): Peterborough
Parking (Coach/Bus): At ground
Police Force and Tel No: Cambridgeshire (01733 563232)
Disabled Visitors' Facilities:
Wheelchairs: South Stand
Blind: No special facility
Future Development(s): The club announced in mid-January that it was examining the possibility of seeking planning permission to replace the existing terraced Moys End Stand with a new 2,000-seat stand as part of a five-year plan that could ultimately see London Road converted into an all-seater stadium.

KEY

C Club Offices
S Club Shop
E Entrance(s) for visiting supporters
R Refreshment bars for visiting supporters
T Toilets for visiting supporters

⬆ North direction (approx)

❶ A15 London Road
❷ Car Parks
❸ Peterborough BR Station (1 mile)
❹ Glebe Road
❺ A605
❻ To A1 (north) (5 miles)
❼ River Nene
❽ To Whittlesey
❾ To A1 (south) (5 miles)
❿ Thomas Cook Stand
⓫ London Road Terrace
⓬ Moys Terrace (away)
⓭ Main Stand

Above: 697321; *Right:* 697312

In late January, it was announced that, despite the team vying for a place in the League Two Play-Offs, manager Mark Wright had been suspended and, a couple of days, later he was sacked for alleged 'gross misconduct'. Earlier in the campaign, Posh had been one of a handful of clubs to suffer the indignity of being knocked out of the FA Cup by non-league opposition when Burton Albion were victorious after a replay. Wright was replaced as caretaker manager by coach Steve Bleasdale, who took over for the remainder of the season. Bleasdale, however, failed to last the course, resigning shortly before the club's 3-2 victory over Macclesfield in late April citing interference from a television programme being made about the club — surely one of the more unusual reasons for club and manager to part company! Barry Fry and Andy Legg took over for the Macclesfield match with the club expecting to make a new appointment imminently; it was, however, not until the end of May that the club announced that ex-Lincoln City boss Keith Alexander would take over for the new season.

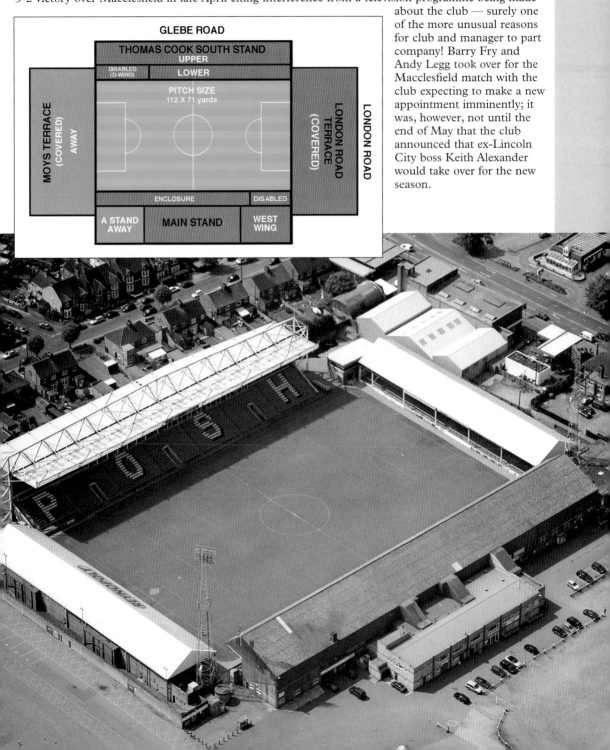

Home Park, Plymouth, PL2 3DQ

Tel No: 01752 562561
Advance Tickets Tel No: 0871 222 1288
Fax: 01752 606167
Web-site: www.pafc.premiumtv.co.uk
E-mail: argyle@pafc.co.uk
League: League Championship
Last Season: 14th (P 46; W 13; D 17; L 16; GF 39; GA 46)
Nickname: The Pilgrims
Brief History: Founded 1886 as Argyle Athletic Club, changed name to Plymouth Argyle in 1903. Founder-members Third Division (1920). Record attendance 43,596
(Total) Current Capacity: 20,134 (15,684 seated)
Visiting Supporters' Allocation: 1,300 (all seated) in Barn Park End Stand up to maximum of 2,000
Club Colours: White and green shirts, green shorts

Nearest Railway Station: Plymouth
Parking (Car): Car park adjacent
Parking (Coach/Bus): Central car park
Police Force and Tel No: Devon & Cornwall (0990 777444)
Disabled Visitors' Facilities:
  Wheelchairs: Devonport End
  Blind: Commentary available
Anticipated Development(s): Work on the three new stands at Home Park progressed well, with work being completed during the 2001/02 season. Plans, however, for the demolition of the existing Main Stand and its replacement have been resurrected as part of a £37 million redevelopment to create a three-tiered structure taking the ground to 18,600 (all-seated). There is no confirmed timescale for this work.

KEY

C Club Offices
S Club Shop

↑ North direction (approx)

❶ A386 Outland Road
❷ Car Park
❸ Devonport Road
❹ Central Park
❺ Town Centre & Plymouth BR Station (¹/₂ mile)
❻ To A38 (½ mile)

Above: 692218; *Right:* 692209

The first managerial casualty once the season started occurred in early September when, after a run of four straight defeats that left the team in 21st position, Argyle sacked Bobby Williamson. After some 18 months in the job, Williamson was replaced as caretaker by Jocky Scott before the club acted quickly and appointed ex-Stoke boss Tony Pulis as manager. Under Pulis Argyle secured their Championship status finishing ultimately in 14th position. Although the Pilgrims possessed one of the meanest defences in the division, the club's primary weakness was in front of goal where only 39 goal were scored all season — exactly the same as the tally for bottom club Brighton. After the end of the season, it was confirmed that Pulis would be returning to Stoke with Ian Holloway being appointed to replace him. Unless Holloway is able to attract a proven goal scorer to Home Park for 2006/07, or improve the strike rate from his existing squad, it looks as though it could be a hard season in Devon to retain the club's Championship status again.

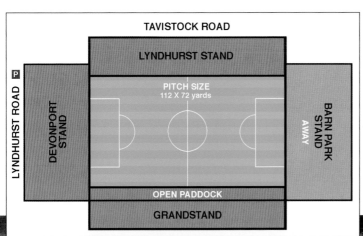

TAVISTOCK ROAD

LYNDHURST STAND

LYNDHURST ROAD

DEVONPORT STAND

PITCH SIZE
112 X 72 yards

BARN PARK STAND
AWAY

OPEN PADDOCK

GRANDSTAND

Fratton Park, 57 Frogmore Road, Portsmouth, Hants, PO4 8RA

Tel No: 02392 731204
Advance Tickets Tel No: 0871 230 1898
Fax: 02392 734129
Web Site: www.pompeyfc.premiumtv.co.uk
E-Mail: info@pompeyfc.co.uk
League: F.A. Premier
Last Season: 17th (P 38; W 10; D 8; L 20; GF 37; GA 62)
Nickname: Pompey
Brief History: Founded 1898. Founder-members Third Division (1920). Record attendance 51,385
(Total) Current Capacity: 20,288 (all seated)
  Visiting Supporters' Allocation: 3,121 (max) in Milton Stand
Club Colours: Blue shirts, white shorts
Nearest Railway Station: Fratton
Parking (Car): Street parking
Parking (Coach/Bus): As directed by Police
Police Force and Tel No: Hampshire (02392 321111)

Disabled Visitors' Facilities:
  Wheelchairs: TY Europe Stand
  Blind: No special facility
Anticipated Development(s): The club was given formal approval by the local authority for the construction of the new ground in late July 2004. The proposed realignment of the ground will have an initial capacity of 28,000 rising to 36,000 if required. The scheme is scheduled to cost £25 million and will be undertaken by Barr Construction. Work is scheduled to start in the summer of 2006 with the redevelopment of the North Stand, with the pitch being rotated at the end of the 2006/07 season. Apart from a new North Stand, work also is planned to include new West and East stands with part of the Leitch-designed South Stand being retained.

PORTSMOUTH

KEY

- **C** Club Offices
- **S** Club Shop
- **E** Entrance(s) for visiting supporters
- **R** Refreshment bars for visiting supporters
- **T** Toilets for visiting supporters

↑ North direction (approx)

❶ Alverstone Road
❷ Carisbrook Road
❸ A288 Milton Road
❹ A2030 Velder Avenue A27
❺ A2030 Goldsmith Avenue
❻ Fratton BR station (½ mile)
❼ TY Europe Stand
❽ Milton End
❾ North Stand
❿ South Stand

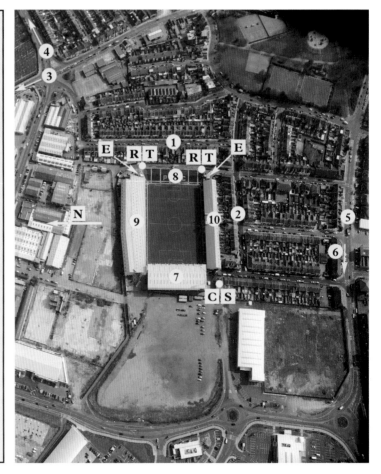

Above: 69908; *Right:* 699898

After several weeks of speculation and a poor start to the season, Alain Perrin was sacked as manager towards the end of November. Only appointed towards the end of the 2004/05 season, Perrin had ensured that Pompey survived in the Premier League at the end of that season, but with only two wins since the start of the 2005/06 campaign the team was just outside the relegation zone following a 3-0 defeat at Liverpool. Following Perrin's departure — the first in the Premier League in the 2005/06 season — Joe Jordan took over as caretaker but erstwhile boss Harry Redknapp made a controversial return to the hot-seat following his resignation as manager of Southampton. Making use of the January transfer window, courtesy of the arrival of new Russian investment (where have we heard of that before?), Redknapp significantly enhanced the quality of the squad but it took some time for the new players to gel and, even in the last few weeks of the season, it looked as though Redknapp was going to earn the unenviable reputation of taking two different clubs down in consecutive seasons. However, a late rally earned Redknapp the 'Houdini' soubriquet as the team secured its Premier League status with victory at Wigan. After the scare in 2005/06 and with the new investment coming through, 2006/07 should be a quieter affair at Fratton Park and Premier League survival should be more easily secured. Whilst Pompey will struggle to be more than a mid-table team, the quality should be there to ensure easy survival.

MILTON LANE

UPPER
NORTH STAND
LOWER

PITCH SIZE
114 X 72 yards

DISABLED FANS

FROGMORE ROAD

TY EUROPE STAND

INTER-CITY CASH
(MILTON) END
AWAY

ASPLEY ROAD

SOUTH STAND

CARISBROOKE ROAD

Vale Park, Burslem, Stoke-on-Trent, ST6 1AW

Tel No: 01782 655800
Advance Tickets Tel No: 01782 655832
Fax: 01782 834981
Web Site: www.port-vale.premiumtv.co.uk
E-Mail: enquiries@port-vale.co.uk
League: League One
Last Season: 13th (P 46; W 16; D 12; L 18; GF 49; GA 54)
Nickname: The Valiants
Brief History: Founded 1876 as Burslem Port Vale, changed name to 'Port Vale' in 1907 (reformed club). Former Grounds: The Meadows Longport, Moorland Road Athletic Ground, Cobridge Athletic Grounds, Recreation Ground Hanley, moved to Vale Park in 1950. Founder-members Second Division (1892). Record attendance 49,768

(Total) Current Capacity: 23,000 (all seated)
Visiting Supporters' Allocation: 4,550 (in Hamil Road [Phones4U] Stand)
Club Colours: White shirts, black shorts
Nearest Railway Station: Longport (two miles)
Parking (Car): Car park at Ground
Parking (Coach/Bus): Hamil Road car park
Police Force and Tel No: Staffordshire (01782 577114)
Disabled Visitors' Facilities:
  Wheelchairs: 20 spaces in new Britannic Disabled Stand
  Blind: Commentary available
Anticipated Development(s): After some years of standing half completed, the club's new owners completed the roof over the Lorne Street Stand during the 2004/05 season.

KEY

E Entrance(s) for visiting supporters

⬆ North direction (approx)

❶ Car Parks
❷ Hamil Road
❸ Lorne Street
❹ To B5051 Moorland Road
❺ To Burslem Town Centre
❻ Railway Stand
❼ Sentinel Stand
❽ Hamil Road Stand
❾ Lorne Street Stand
❿ Family Section

PORT VALE

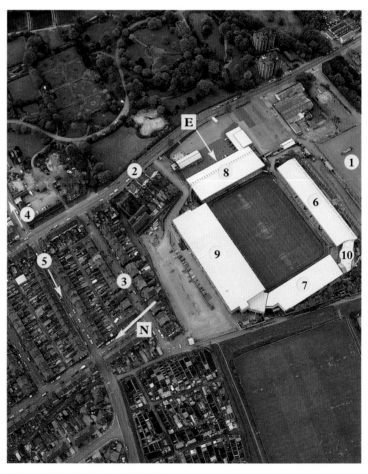

Above: 698939; Right: 698947

Under Martin Foyle, the Valiants made some limited progress on the field in finishing in 13th, as opposed to 18th at the end of the 2004/05 season, although the number of goals scored — 49 — was identical to the total in the league during the earlier season. The improvement in the team's position was largely the result of a much tighter defence and of the failure of a number of other teams to match even the meagre total of 49 goals. If the team is to make significant progress then Foyle undoubtedly needs to attract a proven goal scorer to Vale Park; without this, it's hard to escape the thought that the new campaign could well again see the team struggle to stay above the drop zone.

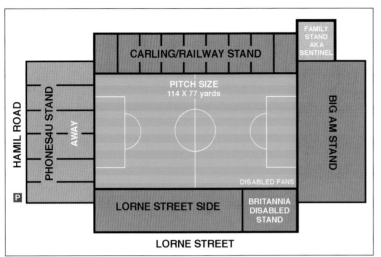

Deepdale, Sir Tom Finney Way, Preston, PR1 6RU

Tel No: 0870 442 1964
Advance Tickets Tel No: 0870 4421966
Fax: 01772 693366
Web Site: www.pnefc.premiumtv.co.uk
E-Mail: enquiries@pne.com
League: League Championship
Last Season: 4th (P 46; W 20; D 20; L 6; GF 59; GA 30)
Nickname: The Lilywhites
Brief History: Founded 1867 as a Rugby Club, changed to soccer in 1881. Former ground: Moor Park, moved to (later named) Deepdale in 1875. Founder-members Football League (1888). Record attendance 42,684
(Total) Current Capacity: 22,225 (all seated)
Visiting Supporters' Allocation: 6,000 maximum in Bill Shankly Stand
Club Colours: White shirts, blue shorts

Nearest Railway Station: Preston (2 miles)
Parking (Car): West Stand car park
Parking (Coach/Bus): West Stand car park
Police Force and Tel No: Lancashire (01772 203203)
Disabled Visitors' Facilities:
  Wheelchairs: Tom Finney Stand and Bill Shankly Stand
  Blind: Earphones Commentary
Anticipated Development(s): With three sides of the ground now rebuilt, the next phase of the redevelopment of Deepdale will involve the reconstruction of the Pavilion Stand. Current plans involve the construction of a single-tier stand accommodating 5,000 to take the ground's capacity to 24,000 although there is no confirmed timescale for this project as yet.

KEY

S Club Shop

⬆ North direction (approx)

❶ A6033 Deepdale Road
❷ Lawthorpe Road
❸ Car Park
❹ A5085 Blackpool Road
❺ Preston BR Station (2 miles)
❻ Bill Shankly Stand
❼ Tom Finney Stand
❽ Town End Stand

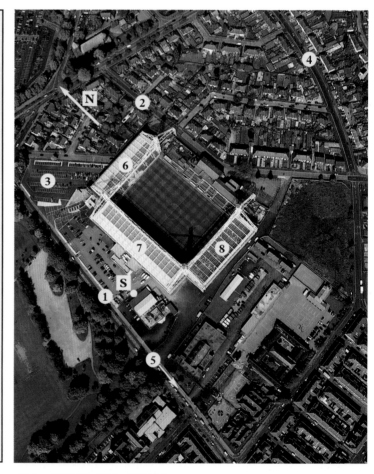

Above: 699138; *Right:* 699139

A season of some promise at Deepdale ended both in the disappointment of losing in the Play-Offs for the second year in succession and then losing manager Billy Davies who left after the end of the season to take over at Derby. In the league, whilst Preston were never strong enough to sustain a serious challenge for the automatic promotion places, the Play-Offs always seemed to be within their grasp and in finishing fourth the club faced Leeds United over the two legs. A 1-1 draw at Elland Road had seemed to give the Lilywhites the edge but in the return leg at Deepdale Preston failed to take their chances, despite Leeds being reduced to nine players by the end of the match, and ultimately lost 2-0 on the night. New manager Paul Simpson will have his work cut out to restore morale within the squad and, with strong teams having come down from the Premier League, it's hard to gainsay the argument that Preston's best chance of a return to the top flight may have disappeared. Provided that Simpson can steady the ship, then a top half finish should be possible but reaching the Play-Offs may be beyond the team's hopes.

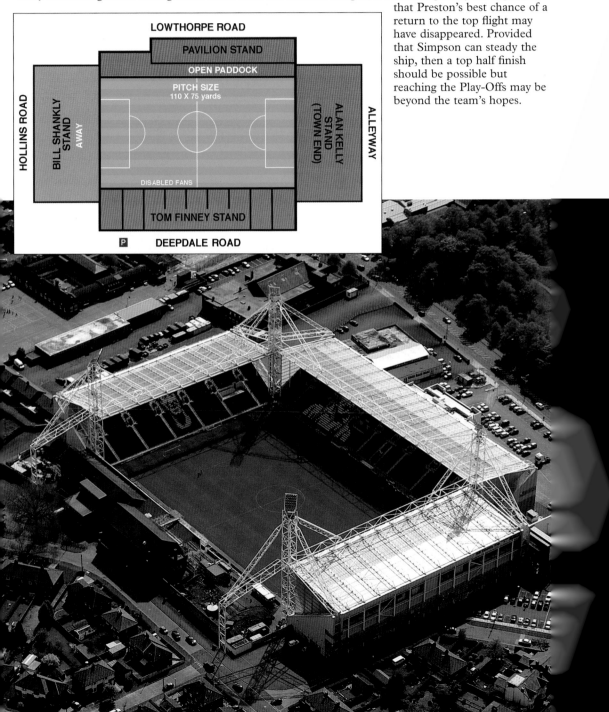

Loftus Road Stadium, South Africa Road, London, W12 7PA

Tel No: 020 8743 0262
Advance Tickets Tel No: 0870 112 1967
Fax: 020 8749 0994
Web Site: www.qpr.premiumtv.co.uk
E-Mail: boxoffice@qpr.co.uk
League: League Championship
Last Season: 21st (P46; W 12; D 14; L 20; GF 50; GA 65)
Nickname: The Superhoops
Brief History: Founded 1885 as 'St. Jude's Institute', amalgamated with Christchurch Rangers to become Queens Park Rangers in 1886. Football League record number of former Grounds and Ground moves (13 different venues, 17 changes), including White City Stadium (twice) final move to Loftus Road in 1963. Founder-members Third Division (1920). Record attendance (at Loftus Road) 35,353
(Total) Current Capacity: 18,500 (all seated)

Visiting Supporters' Allocation: 2,500 (maximum)
Club Colours: Blue and white hooped shirts, white shorts
Nearest Railway Station: Shepherds Bush and White City (both tube)
Parking (Car): White City NCP and street parking
Parking (Coach/Bus): White City NCP
Police Force and Tel No: Metropolitan (020 8741 6212)
Disabled Visitors' Facilities:
Wheelchairs: Ellerslie Road Stand and West Paddock
Blind: Ellerslie Road Stand
Anticipated Development(s): There is vague talk of possible relocation, but nothing has been confirmed. Given the constrained site occupied by Loftus Road, it will be difficult to increase the existing ground's capacity.

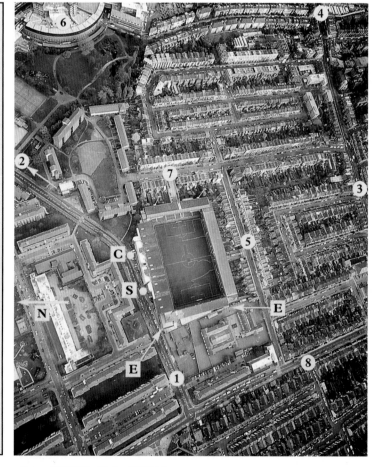

KEY

C Club Offices
S Club Shop
E Entrance(s) for visiting supporters

↑ North direction (approx)

❶ South Africa Road
❷ To White City Tube Station, A219 Wood Lane and A40 Western Avenue
❸ A4020 Uxbridge Road
❹ To Shepherds Bush Tube Station
❺ To Acton Central Station
❻ BBC Television Centre
❼ Loftus Road
❽ Bloemfontein Road

Above: 695957; *Right:* 695948

The managerial vacancy at Leicester City had consequences in west London when it was announced in early February that Ian Holloway had been suspended as manager due to his interest in perhaps taking on the Leicester role. Whilst the club chairman, Gianni Paladini, said that Holloway would not be sacked and that the club would honour his contract in the event of him not being offered the Leicester job, he would not be returning as QPR boss. With Holloway suspended, Gary Waddock took over as caretaker, continuing in the role until the end of the season and being confirmed as permanent boss later. With the uncertainty off the field, the team struggled on it, ultimately finishing in a disappointing 21st place some eight points off relegated Crewe. Although QPR were never actually sucked into the relegation battle, if the season had gone on much longer the team could well have struggled to survive. The club also struggled in the Carling Cup, being defeated 3-0 away at League Two Northampton Town. Unless things improve dramatically for next season, then QPR look as though they'll be a team struggling to retain its place in the League Championship.

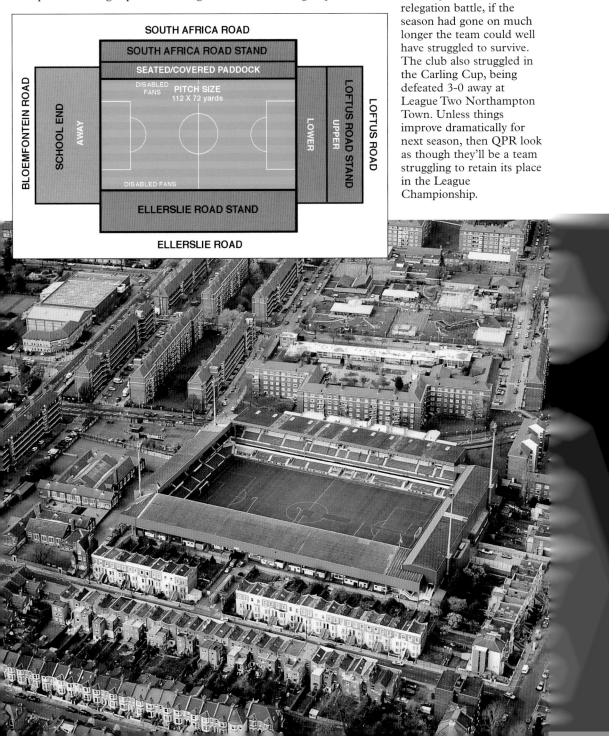

Madejski Stadium, Bennet Road, Reading, RG2 0FL

Tel No: 0118 968 1100
Advance Tickets Tel No: 0870 999 1871
Fax: 0118 968 1101
Web Site: www.readingfc.premiumtv.co.uk
E-Mail: customerservice@readingfc.co.uk
League: F.A. Premier
Last Season: 1st (promoted League Championship) (P46; W 31; D 13; L 2; GF 99; GA 32)
Nickname: The Royals
Brief History: Founded 1871. Amalgamated with Reading Hornets in 1877 and with Earley in 1889. Former Grounds: Reading Recreation Ground, Reading Cricket Ground, Coley Park, Caversham Cricket Cround and Elm Park (1895-1998); moved to the Madejski Stadium at the start of the 1998/99 season. Founder-members of the Third Division in 1920. Record attendance (at Elm Park) 33,042; (at Madejski Stadium) 24,107
(Total) Current Capacity: 24,200 (all seated)
Visiting Supporters' Allocation: 4,500 (maximum in the Fosters Lager South Stand)
Club Colours: White with blue hoops shirts, white shorts
Nearest Railway Station: Reading (2.5 miles)
Parking (Car): 1,800-space car park at the ground, 700 of these spaces are reserved
Parking (Coach/Bus): As directed
Other Clubs Sharing Ground: London Irish RUFC
Police Force and Tel No: Thames Valley (0118 953 6000)
Disabled Visitors' Facilities:
  Wheelchairs: 128 designated spaces on all four sides of the ground
  Blind: 12 places for match day commentaries
Anticipated Development(s): Following the club's promotion to the Premier League at the end of the season, chairman John Madejski announced that, if the club retained its Premier League status at the end of the 2006/07 season, plans would be put in place to increase the ground's capacity to 40,000. There is no timescale for this work other than its dependence on Reading surviving in the Premier League.

KEY

C Club Offices
S Club Shop

↑ North direction (approx)

❶ North Stand
❷ East Stand
❸ South Stand (away)
❹ West Stand
❺ A33 Basingstoke Road
❻ A33 to M4 (Jct 11)
❼ A33 to Reading Town Centre and station (two miles)
❽ Hurst Way
❾ Boot End

Above: 699828; *Right:* 699833

WEST (ULTIMA BUSINESS SOLUTIONS) STAND

UPPER

LOWER

PITCH SIZE
102 X 70 metres

SOUTH (FOSTERS LAGER) STAND AWAY

NORTH (NPOWER) STAND

EAST (KYOCERA MITA) STAND

ACRE ROAD

Although doing his best to dampen expectations during the course of the season at least publicly, Steve Coppell and his Reading team dominated the League Championship to such an extent that it was obvious to many, almost from the start of the campaign, that the team would achieve automatic promotion to the Premier League. Having amassed no fewer than 106 points during the course of a season where they were defeated only twice and having scored no fewer than 99 goals (achieving the remarkable goal difference of +67!), the Royals were promoted well before the end of the campaign and thus achieve top-flight football for the first time in the club's history. Of the three teams promoted at the end of 2005/06, Reading undoubtedly has the greatest potential to do reasonably well at the higher level with a modern ground and a chairman, in John Madejski, able to plough the odd bob in if needed. Steve Coppell is also an astute manager and, therefore, it's likely that the Royals will do a 'Wigan' rather than a 'Sunderland' in their first season at this level.

Willbutts Lane, Spotland Stadium, Rochdale, OL11 5DS

Tel No: 01706 644648
Advance Tickets Tel No: 0870 822 1907
Fax: 01706 648466
Web-site: www.rochdaleafc.premiumtv.co.uk
E-Mail: info@rochdaleafc.co.uk
League: League Two
Last Season: 14th (P46; W 14; D 14; L 18; GF 66; GA 69)
Nickname: The Dale
Brief History: Founded 1907 from former Rochadale Town F.C. (founded 1900). Founder-members Third Division North (1921). Record attendance 24,231
(Total) Current Capacity: 10,262 (8,342 seated) following completion of Pearl Street Stand
Visiting Supporters' Allocation: 3,650 (seated) in Willbutts Lane (Westrose Leisure) Stand

Club Colours: Blue shirts, blue shorts
Nearest Railway Station: Rochdale
Parking (Car): Rear of ground
Parking (Coach/Bus): Rear of ground
Other Clubs Sharing Ground: Rochdale Hornets RLFC
Police Force and Tel No: Greater Manchester (0161 872 5050)
Disabled Visitors' Facilities:
Wheelchairs: Main, WMG and Willbutts Lane stands – disabled area
Blind: Commentary available
Anticipated Development(s): None following completion of Willbutts Lane Stand.

KEY

C Club Offices
S Club Shop
E Entrance(s) for visiting supporters

↑ North direction (approx)

❶ Willbutts Lane
❷ A627 Edenfield Road
❸ Rochdale BR Station (1/2 mile)
❹ Sandy Lane
❺ To M62
❻ To M65 and North
❼ Pearl Street (Westrose Leisure) Stand
❽ Willbutts Lane Stand

ROCHDALE

Above: 696966; *Right:* 696972

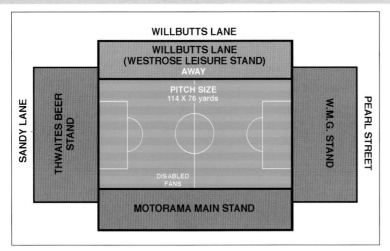

WILLBUTTS LANE

**WILLBUTTS LANE
(WESTROSE LEISURE STAND)
AWAY**

PITCH SIZE
114 X 76 yards

DISABLED FANS

MOTORAMA MAIN STAND

SANDY LANE

THWAITES BEER STAND

W.M.G. STAND

PEARL STREET

In 2004/05 Steve Parkin's team had come within striking distance of the Play-Offs courtesy of a strong defence but an inability to score goals. In 2005/06 the reverse applied; the team was one of the most prolific scorers in the division — no team outside the top six scored as many — but the strikers' efforts were undermined by one of the leakiest defences, with a total of 69 goals conceded. Barely a handful of clubs had as dire a defensive record; even relegated Oxford managed to concede only 57 during the course of the league season. Having come close to the Play-Offs in 2004/05, finishing in 14th position was a considerable disappointment and it's hard to escape the conclusion that Rochdale's more than 30-year presence in the league's basement will not be altered during 2006/07. A position of mid-table mediocrity, at best, is perhaps all that can be hoped for.

Millmoor Ground, Millmoor Lane, Rotherham, S60 1HR

Tel No: 01709 512434
Advance Tickets Tel No: 0870 443 1884
Fax: 01709 512762
Web Site: www.themillers.premiumtv.co.uk
E-Mail: office@rotherhamunited.net
League: League One
Last Season: 20th (P 46; W 12; D 16; L 18; GF 52; GA 62)
Nickname: The Millers
Brief History: Founded 1877 (as Thornhill later Thornhill United), changed name to Rotherham County in 1905 and to Rotherham United in 1925 (amalgamated with Rotherham Town – Football League members 1893-97 – in 1925). Former Grounds include: Red House Ground and Clifton Lane Cricket Ground, moved to Millmoor in 1907. Record attendance 25,170
(Total) Current Capacity: 7,500
　Visiting Supporters' Allocation: 2,155 (all seated) in Railway End

Club Colours: Red shirts, white shorts
Nearest Railway Station: Rotherham Central
Parking (Car): Kimberworth and Main Street car parks, plus large car park adjacent to ground
Parking (Coach/Bus): As directed by Police
Police Force and Tel No: South Yorkshire (01709 371121)
Disabled Visitors' Facilities:
　Wheelchairs: Millmoor Lane
　Blind: Commentary available
Anticipated Developments(s): Despite the problems with the club's finances, which have resulted in a 10 point penalty at the start of the new season, work commenced on the construction of the new 4,200-seat Main Stand during 2006. The £3.3 million scheme should be completed by the early part of the 2006/07 season.

KEY

C Club Offices
S Club Shop
E Entrance(s) for visiting supporters
R Refreshment bars for visiting supporters
T Toilets for visiting supporters

↑ North direction (approx)

❶ Main Stand
❷ To Rotherham Central BR Station
❸ A6109 Masborough Street
❹ Millmoor Lane
❺ To A6178 and M1 Junction 34
❻ A630 Centenary Way
❼ Station Road

Above: 699921; *Right:* 699925

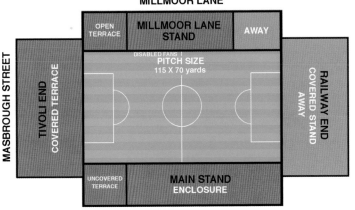

MILLMOOR LANE

| OPEN TERRACE | MILLMOOR LANE STAND | AWAY |

MASBROUGH STREET

TIVOLI END COVERED TERRACE

DISABLED FANS
PITCH SIZE
115 X 70 yards

RAILWAY END COVERED STAND AWAY

| UNCOVERED TERRACE | MAIN STAND ENCLOSURE |

Following a run of 17 league and cup games without a victory, culminating in a 2-1 home defeat against Yeovil that left the Millers rooted in the League One relegation zone, manager Mick Harford was sacked in early December. For the second time in his career Alan Knill was appointed caretaker, with the position made permanent in mid-January. Under Knill, the club was able to retain its League One status — but only just as it required results on the final day to go the Millers' way if the club was to survive. Effectively it came down to the match at Millmoor with relegation rivals MK Dons. Whoever lost was relegated but, in the event, a 0-0 draw was enough to keep Rotherham up by two points. At the end of the season, however, it was announced that, as the club had sought an arrangement with its creditors to avoid receivership, the Millers would start the 2006/07 season with a minus 10-point penalty. The last team to suffer such a fate, Wrexham, was ultimately relegated and it's hard to escape the conclusion that, with this penalty, United will not survive the drop again.

Glanford Park, Doncaster Road, Scunthorpe DN15 8TD

Tel No: 01724 848077
Advance Tickets Tel No: 01724 848077
Fax: 01724 857986
Web Site: www.scunthorpe-united.premiumtv.co.uk
E-mail: admin@scunthorpe-united.co.uk
League: League One
Last Season: 12th (P 46; W 15; D 15; L 16; GF 68; GA 73)
Nickname: The Iron
Brief History: Founded 1899 as Scunthorpe United, amalgamated with North Lindsey to become 'Scunthorpe & Lindsey United' in 1912. Changed name to Scunthorpe United in 1956. Former Grounds: Crosby (Lindsey United) and Old Showground, moved to Glanford Park in 1988. Elected to Football League in 1950. Record attendance 8,775 (23,935 at Old Showground)
(Total) Current Capacity: 9,200 (6,400 seated)

Visiting Supporters' Allocation: 1,678 (all seated) in South (Caparo Merchant Bar) Stand
Club Colours: Claret and blue shirts, claret shorts
Nearest Railway Station: Scunthorpe
Parking (Car): At ground
Parking (Coach/Bus): At ground
Police Force and Tel No: Humberside (01724 282888)
Disabled Visitors' Facilities:
  Wheelchairs: County Chef Stand
  Blind: Commentary available
Anticipated Development(s): Although a new stadium – Glanford Park opened in 1988 – there is a possibility that, in the future, the existing Evening Telegraph Stand will be demolished and replaced by a two-tier structure.

KEY

C Club Offices
S Club Shop
E Entrance(s) for visiting supporters
R Refreshment bars for visiting supporters
T Toilets for visiting supporters

↑ North direction (approx)

❶ Car Park
❷ Evening Telegraph Stand
❸ A18 to Scunthorpe BR Station and Town Centre (1½ miles)
❹ M181 and M180 Junction 3

Above: 697516; Right: 697507

146

EVENING TELEGRAPH STAND

PITCH SIZE
111 X 73 yards

SOUTH STAND

AWAY

DON CASS COMMUNITY STAND

TERRACE

DISABLED FANS

COUNTY CHEF STAND

Although the season started disappointingly with Brian Laws' team struggling towards the bottom half of the table having been promoted at the end of the 2004/05 campaign, eventually the team achieved a creditable 12th position thereby consolidating its position in League One and laying the foundation for a more sustained challenge on the top half of the division in the new season. One concern for Laws will be the number of goals conceded as the Iron had no problems finding the opponents' net; in terms of goals scored, Scunthorpe would easily have finished in a Play-Off position but in terms of goals conceded the team had probably the worst record in League One.

Bramall Lane, Sheffield, S2 4SU

Tel No: 0870 787 1960
Advance Tickets Tel No: 0870 787 1799
Fax: 0870 787 3345
Web Site: www.sufc.premiumtv.co.uk
E-Mail: info@sufc.co.uk
League: F.A. Premiership
Last Season: 2nd (promoted) (P46; W 26; D 12; L 8; GF 76; GA 46)
Nickname: The Blades
Brief History: Founded 1889. (Sheffield Wednesday occasionally used Bramall Lane c1880.) Founder-members 2nd Division (1892). Record attendance 68,287
(Total) Current Capacity: 33,000 (all seated)
Visiting Supporters' Allocation: 2,700 (seated) can be increased to 5,200 if needed
Club Colours: Red and white striped shirts, black shorts
Nearest Railway Station: Sheffield Midland

Parking (Car): Street parking
Parking (Coach/Bus): As directed by Police
Police Force and Tel No: South Yorkshire (0114 276 8522)
Disabled Visitors' Facilities:
  Wheelchairs: South Stand
  Blind: Commentary available
Anticipated Development(s): Following the completion of the corner stand between the Bramall and Laver stands, which takes the ground's capacity to 33,000, the next phase in the development of Bramall Lane will be the reconstruction of the Hallam FM (Kop) Stand. This two-tiered structure is designed to add 4,000 seats to the ground's capacity. Planning Permission has also been granted for the construction of a 146-bedroom hotel behind the recently constructed corner stand.

KEY

C Club Offices
S Club Shop
E Entrance(s) for visiting supporters

↑ North direction (approx)

❶ A621 Bramall Lane
❷ Shoreham Street
❸ Car Park
❹ Sheffield Midland BR Station (1/4 mile)
❺ John Street
❻ Hallam FM (Kop) Stand
❼ John Street Stand
❽ Bramall Lane (Gordon Lamb) Stand
❾ Laver (South) Stand

SHEFFIELD UNITED

Above: 699964; *Right:* 699967

After several near misses, 2005/06 finally saw Neil Warnock's Sheffield United achieve promotion to the Premier League. Vying at the start of the season with Reading for the top spot, a mid-season blip saw the Blades drop off the pace for the Championship title and revive hopes amongst the chasing pack, most notably Leeds United and Watford, that once again United would blow their chances. In the event, however, United were to gain the second automatic promotion spot well before the end of the campaign and can now look forward to hosting Chelsea and Manchester United rather than Colchester and Southend. The last time Stuart McCall marked promotion to the Premier League — with Bradford City in 1999 — he injured himself during his celebrations thereby missing the start of the season; now Warnock's assistant at Bramall Lane, he brings considerable Premier League experience to a club that will need to call upon every bit of experience that it has in order to survive. Away from the league, however, United suffered the indignity of being knocked out of the FA Cup at Bramall Lane by League One side Colchester United in the third round. As with other promoted teams, United will undoubtedly be one of the pre-season favourites for the drop and it's hard to escape the conclusion that 17th place will be considered a triumph.

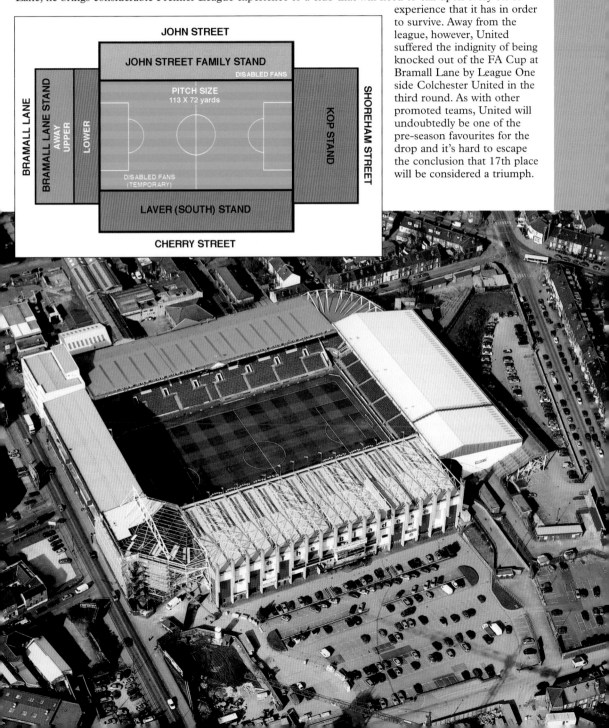

Hillsborough, Sheffield, S6 1SW

Tel No: 0870 999 1867
Advance Tickets Tel No: 0870 999 1867
Fax: 0114 221 2122
Web Site: www.swfc.premiumtv.co.uk
E-Mail: enquiries@swfc.co.uk
League: League Championship
Last Season: 19th (P 46; W 13; D 13; L 20; GF 39; GA 52)
Nickname: The Owls
Brief History: Founded 1867 as The Wednesday F.C. (changed to Sheffield Wednesday c1930). Former Grounds: London Road, Wyrtle Road (Heeley), Sheaf House Ground, Encliffe & Olive Grove (Bramall Lane also used occasionally), moved to Hillsborough (then named 'Owlerton' in 1899). Founder-members Second Division (1892). Record attendance 72,841

(Total) Current Capacity: 39,859 (all seated)
Visiting Supporters' Allocation: 3,700 (all seated) in West Stand Upper
Club Colours: Blue and white striped shirts, black shorts
Nearest Railway Station: Sheffield (2 miles)
Parking (Car): Street Parking
Parking (Coach/Bus): Owlerton Stadium
Police Force and Tel No: South Yorkshire (0114 276 8522)
Disabled Visitors' Facilities:
  Wheelchairs: North and Lower West Stands
  Blind: Commentary available

KEY

C Club Offices
E Entrance(s) for visiting supporters

⬆ North direction (approx)

❶ Leppings Lane
❷ River Don
❸ A61 Penistone Road North
❹ Sheffield BR Station and City Centre (2 miles)
❺ Spion Kop
❻ To M1 (North)
❼ To M1 (South)
❽ West Stand

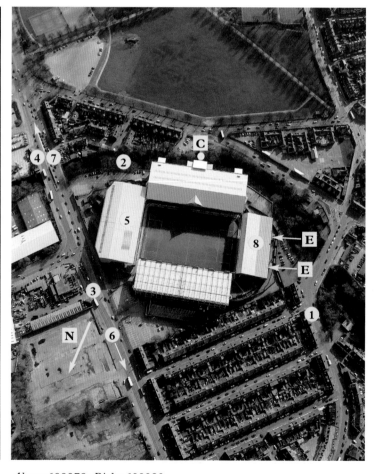

Above: 699978; *Right:* 699980

Promoted at the end of 2004/05, consolidation in the League Championship was Paul Sturrock's primary aim for his Wednesday outfit during 2005/06 and, in this ambition, he was successful. Hovering just above the drop zone for much of the campaign, Wednesday benefited from the fact that, ultimately, the three relegated teams were never strong enough to put together a string of decent results; each of them had a period where they looked capable of escaping the drop, only for form to lapse again. Whilst Wednesday possessed one of the meanest defences in the bottom half of the table, Sturrock will be concerned by his team's inability to score goals. The Owls scored a grand total of 39 in the 46 league games; only relegated Millwall scored fewer. Unless Sturrock is able to strengthen his squad with a proven goal scorer during the summer, it's hard to escape the view that Wednesday will be facing another battle to avoid the drop in 2006/07.

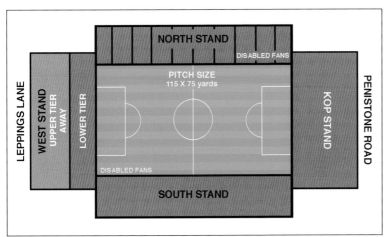

NORTH STAND

DISABLED FANS

PITCH SIZE
115 X 75 yards

LEPPINGS LANE

WEST STAND

UPPER TIER
AWAY

LOWER TIER

PENISTONE ROAD

KOP STAND

DISABLED FANS

SOUTH STAND

Gay Meadow, Shrewsbury, SY2 6AB

Tel No: 01743 360111
Advance Tickets Tel No: 01743 360111
Fax: 01743 236384
Web-site: www.shrewsburytown.co.uk
E-mail: ian@shrewsburytown.co.uk
League: League Two
Last Season: 10th (P 46; W 16; D 13; L 17; GF 55; GA 55)
Nickname: The Shrews
Brief History: Founded 1886. Former Grounds: Monkmoor Racecourse, Ambler's Field and The Barracks Ground (moved to Gay Meadow 1910). Elected to Football League 1950; relegated to Nationwide Conference at end of 2002/03 and promoted back to the Football League, via the Play-Offs, at the end of 2003/04. Record attendance 18,917
(Total) Current Capacity: 8,000 (2,500 seated)
Visiting Supporters' Allocation: 2,500 (500 seated) in the Station End (standing) and Main Stand (seated)

Club Colours: Blue shirts and blue shorts
Nearest Railway Station: Shrewsbury
Parking (Car): Adjacent car park
Parking(Coach/Bus): Gay Meadow
Police Force and Tel No: West Mercia (01743 232888)
Disabled Visitors' Facilities:
  Wheelchairs: Alongside pitch (as directed)
  Blind: No special facility
Anticipated Development(s): After many delays, work has finally started on the construction of the new £15 million ground on Oteley Road with the intention that facilities at the new site will be sufficiently advanced to allow the club to relocate from Gay Meadow at the start of the 2007/08 season. The existing ground will then be redeveloped for housing — a sad loss for all who enjoy slightly quirky football grounds.

SHREWSBURY TOWN

KEY

C Club Offices
S Club Shop
E Entrance(s) for visiting supporters
R Refreshment bars for visiting supporters
T Toilets for visiting supporters

↑ North direction (approx)

❶ Entrance road to ground
❷ Abbey Foregate
❸ River Severn
❹ Car Parks
❺ Shrewsbury BR Station (1 mile – shortest route)
❻ Riverside Terrace
❼ English Bridge
❽ Wyle Cop
❾ Station End (away)
❿ Wakeman End
⓫ Wakeman/Centre/Station Stand
⓬ Old Potts Way (all routes via ring road)

Above: 697458; Right: 697454

Under Gary Peters, the Shrews retained an outside chance of the Play-Offs until virtually the end of the season although a poor start to the campaign meant that they were always, ultimately, going to be a few points behind the pace. However, finishing in 10th place marked a considerable advance on the position achieved in 2004/05 — the team's first season back in the League after a one-year sojourn in the Conference — and, if similar progress can be maintained in 2006/07, there is every possibility that the club could mark its first season in its new ground by playing League One football. Whilst the automatic promotion places may be beyond the team's ability, the Play-Offs should be certainly within reach. The new season will, however, be faced without Joe Hart; the England Under-19 goalkeeper was transferred to Manchester City for a deal that could ultimately bring £1.5 million to the Shrews during the summer.

The Friends Provident St Mary's Stadium, Britannia Road, Southampton SO14 5FP

Tel No: 0870 22 00 000
Advance Tickets Tel No: 0870 2200150
Fax: 02380 727727
Web Site: www.saintsfc.co.uk
E-Mail: tellrupert@saintsfc.co.uk
League: League Championship
Last Season: 12th (P46; W 13; D 19; L 14; GF 49; GA 50)
Nickname: The Saints
Brief History: Founded 1885 as 'Southampton St. Mary's Young Men's Association (changed name to Southampton in 1897). Former Grounds: Northlands Road, Antelope Ground, County Ground, moved to The Dell in 1898 and to St Mary's Stadium in 2001. Founder members Third Division (1920). Record attendance (at The Dell) 31,044 (at St Mary's) 32,151
(Total) Current Capacity: 32,251 (all-seated)

Visiting Supporters' Allocation: c3,200 in North Stand (can be increased to 4,750 if required)
Club Colours: Red and white shirts, black shorts
Nearest Railway Station: Southampton Central
Parking (Car): Street parking or town centre car parks
Parking (Coach/Bus): As directed by the police
Police Force and Tel No: Hampshire (02380 335444)
Disabled Visitors' Facilities:
Wheelchairs: c200 places
Blind: Commentary available
Anticipated Development(s): Following completion of the new stadium the club has no further plans at present.

KEY
C Club Offices
S Club Shop
E Entrance(s) for visiting supporters

↑ North direction (approx)

❶ A3024 Northam Road
❷ B3028 Britannia Road
❸ River Itchen
❹ To M27 (five miles)
❺ To Southampton Central station and town centre
❻ Marine Parade
❼ To A3025 (and Itchen toll bridge)
❽ Belvedere Road
❾ North Stand

Above: 699202; *Right:* 699209

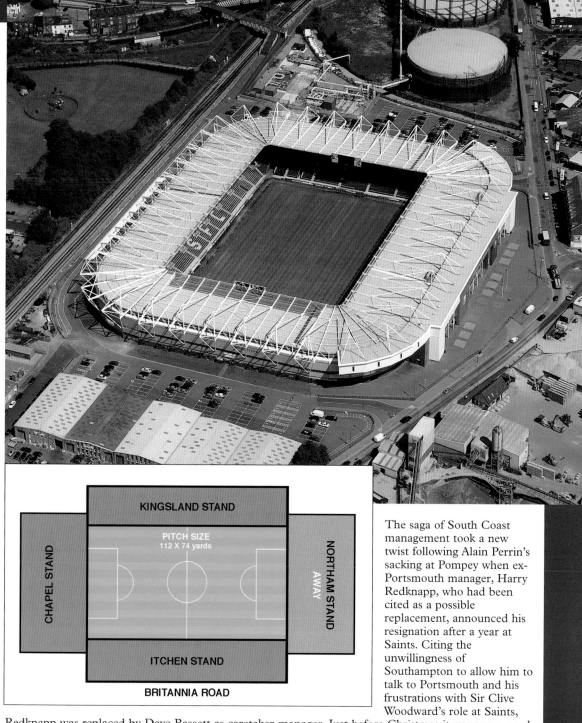

KINGSLAND STAND

PITCH SIZE
112 X 74 yards

CHAPEL STAND

NORTHAM STAND
AWAY

ITCHEN STAND

BRITANNIA ROAD

The saga of South Coast management took a new twist following Alain Perrin's sacking at Pompey when ex-Portsmouth manager, Harry Redknapp, who had been cited as a possible replacement, announced his resignation after a year at Saints. Citing the unwillingness of Southampton to allow him to talk to Portsmouth and his frustrations with Sir Clive Woodward's role at Saints, Redknapp was replaced by Dave Bassett as caretaker-manager. Just before Christmas it was announced that Sir Clive Woodward, the ex-England rugby chief whose presence at the club was one factor in Redknapp's decision, had taken over as Director of Football with ex-Ipswich and Derby boss George Burley as Head Coach. Under Burley, the Saints achieved a position of mid-table safety — tight in defence, weak in front of goal and one of the League Championship's draw specialists. Almost exactly equidistant between the drop zone and the Play-Off in point terms, Saints could well be a team to watch in the 2006/07 season; potentially, Play-Off candidates, but much will depend on who Burley recruits during the summer and whether the off-field battle amongst shareholders is resolved.

Roots Hall Ground, Victoria Avenue, Southend-on-Sea, SS2 6NQ

Tel No: 01702 304050
Advance Tickets Tel No: 01702 304117
Fax: 01702 304124
Web Site: www.southendunited.premiumtv.co.uk
E-mail: info@southend-united.co.uk
League: League Championship
Last Season: 1st (promoted) (P46; W 23; D 13; L 10; GF 72; GA 43)
Nickname: The Shrimpers
Brief History: Founded 1906. Former Grounds: Roots Hall, Kursaal, the Stadium Grainger Road, moved to Roots Hall (new Ground) 1955. Founder-members Third Division (1920). Record attendance 31,033
(Total) Current Capacity: 12,392 (all seated)
Visiting Supporters' Allocation: 2,700 (maximum) (all seated) in North Stand and North West Enclosure

Club Colours: Blue shirts, blue shorts
Nearest Railway Station: Prittlewell
Parking (Car): Street parking
Parking (Coach/Bus): Car park at Ground
Police Force and Tel No: Essex (01702 431212)
Disabled Visitors' Facilities:
  Wheelchairs: West Stand
  Blind: Commentary available
Anticipated Development(s): In early May 2004 it was announced that the local council had backed plans for the construction of the proposed new 16,000-seat stadium costing £12.5 million. The club is now awaiting final planning permission for the construction of the new ground at Fossetts Farm. At this stage, there is no timescale, but it would certainly appear that after some years of uncertainty that Roots Hall is now living on borrowed time.

KEY

C Club Offices
E Entrance(s) for visiting supporters
R Refreshment bars for visiting supporters
T Toilets for visiting supporters

⬆ North direction (approx)

❶ Director's Car Park
❷ Prittlewell BR Station (¼ mile)
❸ A127 Victoria Aveneue
❹ Fairfax Drive
❺ Southend centre (½ mile)
❻ North (Universal Cycles) Stand

Above: 697297; *Right:* 697286

SHAKESPEARE DRIVE

C2C WEST STAND

AWAY

DISABLED FANS

PITCH SIZE
110 X 74 yards

ROOTS HALL AVENUE

HI-TEC (SOUTH) STAND

UPPER TIER

LOWER TIER

NORTH STAND

AWAY

FAIRFAX DRIVE

VISUALLY IMPAIRED

BLACK | GREEN | RED | YELLOW | BLUE

GKC EAST STAND

VICTORIA AVENUE

Promoted to League One at the end of the 2004/05 season, many expected the Shrimpers to take a season to adjust to football at the higher level particularly as the promotion had been achieved through the Play-Offs. In the event, however, courtesy of one of the meanest defences in the Football League, Steve Tilson's team secured promotion well before the end of the season and were ultimately to be crowned well deserved champions following results on the final Saturday when Southend beat Bristol City 1-0 and Colchester could only draw 0-0 away at Yeovil. With two promotions achieved in successive seasons, Southend now face Championship football and visits from Leeds United, West Bromwich Albion and Sunderland rather than Hartlepool, Rotherham and Chesterfield. Given the rapid rise of the team over the past two seasons, it's hard to escape the conclusion that just surviving in the Championship will be considered a triumph amongst the Roots Hall faithful.

Edgeley Park, Hardcastle Road, Edgeley, Stockport, SK3 9DD

Tel No: 0161 286 8888
Advance Tickets Tel No: 0161 286 8888
Fax: 0161 286 8900
Web Site: www.stockportcounty.premiumtv.co.uk
E-Mail: fans@stockportcounty.com
League: League Two
Last Season: 22nd (P46; W 11; D 19; L 16; GF 57; GA 78)
Nickname: The Hatters
Brief History: Founded 1883 as Heaton Norris Rovers, changed name to Stockport County in 1890. Former Grounds: Heaton Norris Recreation Ground, Heaton Norris Wanderers Cricket Ground, Chorlton's Farm, Ash Inn Ground, Wilkes Field (Belmont Street) and Nursery Inn (Green Lane), moved to Edgeley Park in 1902. Record attendance 27,833
(Total) Current Capacity: 11,000 (all seated)
Visiting Supporters' Allocation: 800 (all seated) in Vernon Stand (can be increased by 1,500 all-seated on open Railway End if needed)
Club Colours: Blue with white stripe shirts, blue shorts
Nearest Railway Station: Stockport
Parking (Car): Street Parking
Parking (Coach/Bus): As directed by Police
Other Clubs Sharing Ground: Sale Sharks RUFC
Police Force and Tel No: Greater Manchester (0161 872 5050)
Disabled Visitors' Facilities:
Wheelchairs: Main and Cheadle stands
Blind: Headsets available
Anticipated Development(s): Although the club is still planning for the reconstruction of the Railway End, with the intention of constructing a new 5,500-seat capacity stand on the site, there is no time scale for this work (which had originally been planned for 1999/2000). Theoretically, the next phase after the Railway End would be an upgrade to the Vernon BS Stand, with the intention of making the ground's capacity 20,000.

STOCKPORT COUNTY

KEY
C Club Offices
E Entrance(s) for visiting supporters

↑ North direction (approx)

❶ Mercian Way
❷ Hardcastle Road
❸ Stockport BR station (1/4 mile)
❹ Railway End
❺ Main Stand
❻ Cheadle Stand
❼ Vernon BS Stand

Above: 695712; *Right:* 695706

VERNON BS STAND

AWAY

PITCH SIZE
111 X 71 yards

RAILWAY END
UNCOVERED TERRACE

CHEADLE STAND

DISABLED
FANS

MAIN STAND

P **HARDCASTLE ROAD**

Relegated at the end of 2004/05, Chris Turner's Stockport County should have been able to make a reasonable attempt at League Two football. In the event, however, a dismal first half of the campaign saw the Hatters rooted to the bottom of the League Two table and, following a 6-0 reverse at fellow strugglers Macclesfield Town, Turner departed from the club after some 12 months in the job just after Christmas. The club appointed ex-player Jim Gannon as caretaker initially with the appointment being confirmed until the end of the season in mid-January. Under Gannon, the Hatters secured their League Two status — but only just. Ultimately, the club's fate depended upon results on the last day of the season as one of some five teams could have joined Rushden & Diamonds in the drop to the Conference. In the event, Stockport's 0-0 draw at home to Champions-elect Carlisle allied to Oxford United's defeat to Leyton Orient ensured that County stayed up. However, whilst having a reasonable record at home, the club's abysmal defensive record — the worst in League Two — with some 78 goals conceded means that the club could well struggle again in 2006/07 unless these frailties are sorted out during the close season.

Britannia Stadium, Stanley Matthews Way, Stoke-on-Trent ST4 4EG

Tel No: 01782 592222
Advance Tickets Tel No: 01782 592200
Fax: 01782 592221
Web Site: www.stokecityfc.premiumtv.co.uk
E-Mail: info@stokecityfc.com
League: League Championship
Last Season: 13th (P46; W 17; D 7; L 22; GF 54; GA 63)
Nickname: The Potters
Brief History: Founded 1863 as Stoke F.C., amalgamated with Stoke Victoria in 1878, changed to Stoke City in 1925. Former Grounds: Sweetings Field, Victoria Ground (1878-1997), moved to new ground for start of 1997/98 season. Record attendance (at Victoria Ground): 51,380; at Britannia Stadium 28,218
(Total) Current Capacity: 28,218 (all-seater)
Visiting Supporters' Allocation: 4,800 (in the South Stand)
Club Colours: Red and white striped shirts, white shorts

Nearest Railway Station: Stoke-on-Trent
Parking (Car): The 650 parking spaces at the ground are for officials and guests only. The 1,600 spaces in the South car park are pre-booked only, with the majority held by season ticket holders. There is some on-street parking, but with a 10-15min walk.
Parking (Coach/Bus): As directed
Police Force and Tel No: Staffordshire (01782 744644)
Disabled Visitors' Facilities:
　Wheelchairs: 164 places for disabled spectators
　Blind: Commentaries available
Anticipated Development(s): There are long-term plans to increase the ground's to 30,000 by the construction of a corner stand between the John Smith Stand and the Boothen End but there is no timescale for this work.

KEY

⬆ North direction (approx)

❶ A50
❷ To Stoke BR station
❸ To A500 Queensway and City Centre, railway station and M6
❹ North Stand
❺ West Stand
❻ East Stand
❼ South Stand (away)
❽ To Uttoxeter

Above: 698966; *Right:* 698973

Under Johan Boskamp, appointed just before the start of the 2005/06 season, the Potters finished in 13th place (as opposed to 12th the year before, and 11th the year before that — at the current rate of progress, City should be worried about its Championship status in about a decade's time!). However, events on the field were overshadowed by events off it as the club's Icelandic owners sold out to a new locally-based consortium headed by director Peter Coates, who promised to inject some £8.3 million into stabilising the club's finances, and Boskamp announced that he wouldn't be staying at the Britannia Stadium for the 2006/07 season as the deal on offer was not satisfactory. Following

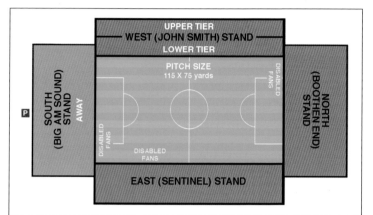

Boskamp's departure, announced after the final game of the season (a 5-1 drubbing of relegated Brighton), the club agreed terms with Plymouth to allow ex-manager Tony Pulis to return. With the club's finances potentially restored there is every possibility that under Pulis the club can secure a top-half finish in 2006/07 although the Play-Offs look more of a pipe-dream.

Stadium of Light, Sunderland, SR5 1SU

Tel No: 0191 551 5000
Advance Tickets Tel No: 0845 671 1973
Fax: 0191 551 5123
Web Site: www.safc.com
E-Mail: Via Website
League: F.A. Premier
Last Season: 20th (relegated Premier League) (P 38; W 3; D 6; L 29; GF 26; GA 69)
Nickname: Black Cats
Brief History: Founded 1879 as 'Sunderland & District Teachers Association', changed to 'Sunderland Association' in 1880 and shortly after to 'Sunderland'. Former Grounds: Blue House Field, Groves Field (Ashbrooke), Horatio Street, Abbs Field, Newcastle Road and Roker Park (1898-1997); moved to Stadium of Light for the start of the 1997/98 season. Record crowd (at Roker Park): 75,118; at Stadium of Light (48,353)
(Total) Current Capacity: 48,353 all-seater
Visiting Supporters' Allocation: 3,000 (South Stand)
Club Colours: Red and white striped shirts, black shorts

Nearest Railway Station: Stadium of Light (Tyne & Wear Metro
Parking (Car): Car park at ground reserved for season ticket holders. Limited on-street parking (but the police may decide to introduce restrictions). Otherwise off-street parking in city centre
Parking (Coach/Bus): As directed
Police Force and Tel No: Tyne & Wear (0191 510 2020)
Disabled Visitors' Facilities:
Wheelchairs: 180 spots
Blind: Commentary available
Anticipated Development(s): The club has long term plans to increase capacity at the Stadium of Light by 7,200 in an expanded Metro FM Stand and a further 9,000 in a second tier to the McEwans Stand, taking the ultimate capacity of the ground to 64,000. There is, however, no confirmed timescale and much will depend on the club regaining — and retaining! — a place in the Premier League.

KEY

C Club Offices
S Club Shop
E Entrance(s) for visiting supporters

⬆ North direction (approx)

❶ River Wear
❷ North (McEwans) Stand
❸ South (Metro FM) Stand (away)
❹ To Sunderland BR station (0.5 mile)
❺ Southwick Road
❻ Stadium Way
❼ Millennium Way
❽ Hay Street
❾ To Wearmouth Bridge (via A1018 North Bridge Street) to City Centre

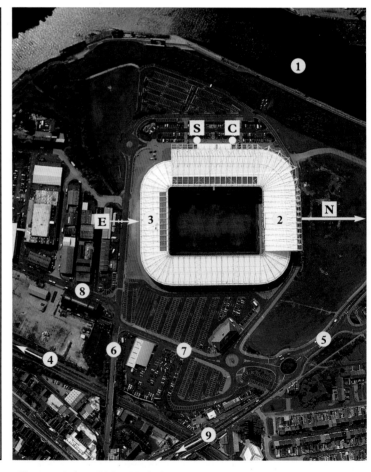

Above: 699151; *Right:* 699159

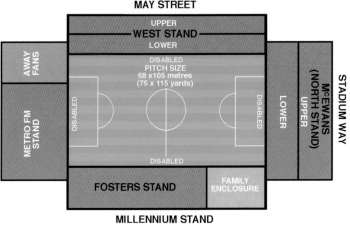

MAY STREET		
UPPER **WEST STAND** LOWER		
DISABLED PITCH SIZE 68 x105 metres (75 x 115 yards)		
AWAY FANS	DISABLED	DISABLED	LOWER UPPER McEWANS (NORTH STAND) STADIUM WAY
METRO FM STAND		
DISABLED		
FOSTERS STAND	FAMILY ENCLOSURE	
MILLENNIUM STAND		

Although the other two clubs promoted at the end of the 2004/05 season prospered in the Premier League, Sunderland struggled and, in early March following a 2-1 defeat at Manchester City, which left the team rooted to the bottom on the table with a total of 10 points from 28 games, Mick McCarthy was sacked as manager. Away from the league, the club's disappointing form continued with a 2-1 defeat in the fourth round of the FA Cup at League One Brentford. By that stage of the season, with only 10 games left, the Black Cats were already 16 points from safety and so caretaker boss, Kevin Ball, had only two real aims left: to restore some pride to the team and endeavour to try and overhaul the total of points achieved when Sunderland last played in the Premier League. Unfortunately, whilst the former might have been achieved to a limited extent — a draw at Manchester United being the high point; a 4-1 defeat at home by Newcastle being the low — the latter wasn't. With a grand total of only 15 points, Sunderland have set a new benchmark (although they did finally achieve a solitary league win at home at the end of the season). The new manager, Niall Quinn, should retain the bulk of the quad and so a challenge for automatic promotion should be likely although things may be complicated by a take-over struggle for the club with ex-star Niall Quinn fronting a consortium to oust chairman Bob Murray.

Liberty Stadium, Morfa, Swansea SA1 2FA

Telephone: 01792 616600
Advance Tickets Tel No: 0870 040004
Fax: 01792 616606
Web site: www.swanseacity.premiumtv.co.uk
E-mail: dawn@swanseacityfc.co.uk
League: League One
Last Season: 6th (P 46; W 18; D 17; L 11; GF 78; GA 55)
Nickname: The Swans
Brief History: Founded 1900 as Swansea Town, changed to Swansea City in 1970. Former grounds: various, including Recreation Ground, and Vetch Field (1912-2005); moved to the new ground for the start of the 2005/06 season. Founder-members Third Division (1920). Record attendance (at Vetch Field): 32,796; (at Liberty Stadium) 19,288.
(Total) Current Capacity: 20,500
Visiting Supporters' Allocation: 3,500 maximum in North Stand

Club Colours: white shirts, white shorts
Nearest Railway Station: Swansea
Parking (Car): Adjacent to ground
Parking (Coach/Bus): As directed
Other Clubs Sharing Ground: Swansea Ospreys RUFC
Police Force and Tel No: South Wales (01792 456999)
Disabled Visitors' Facilities:
Wheelchairs: tbc
Blind: tbc
Anticipated Development(s): After several years of uncertainty, Swansea City relocated to the new White Rock Stadium with its 20,000 all-seater capacity for the start of the 2005/06 season. The ground, which cost £27 million to construct and which was built near the site of the old Morfa stadium, is shared by the Swansea Ospreys RUFC team.

KEY

⬆ North direction (approx)

❶ A4067 Ffordd Cwm Tawe Road
❷ A4067 to A48 and M4 Junction 44 (five miles)
❸ B4603 Neath Road
❹ Brunel Way
❺ Normandy Road
❻ A4217
❼ To Swansea city centre and BR railway station (two miles)
❽ Parking
❾ Cardiff-Swansea railway line

Above: 700168; *Right:* 700180

Promoted at the end of 2004/05 and with a brand-new stadium to mark the club's arrival in League One, optimism was high at the Liberty Stadium — and with good reason. Under Kenny Jackett the team prospered, becoming the division's highest scorers with no fewer than 78 goals, and, for much of the campaign it looked as though automatic promotion was a possibility. In the event, however, a dip in form meant that it came down to the final Saturday of the season as to whether the Swans retained a place in the Play-Offs. With four teams — Barnsley, Forest and Doncaster being the other three — all competing for the remaining two places. In the event, a crushing 4-0 victory over Chesterfield at Saltergate ensured that Swansea finished in sixth place and thus faced Brentford in the Play-Offs. A 1-1 draw at the Liberty Stadium seemed to give Brentford the edge but a superb 2-0 victory at Griffin Park saw Swansea progress to the final — their second of the season having earlier won the LDV trophy — where Barnsley lay in wait. Unfortunately, it proved a game too far for Jackett's team as Barnsley won on penalties after the game ended in a 2-2 draw. Thus 2006/07 will again see Swansea in League one but provided that Jackett can retain the bulk of his squad, including prolific scorer Lee Trundell, then the Swans should again feature in the chase for automatic promotion.

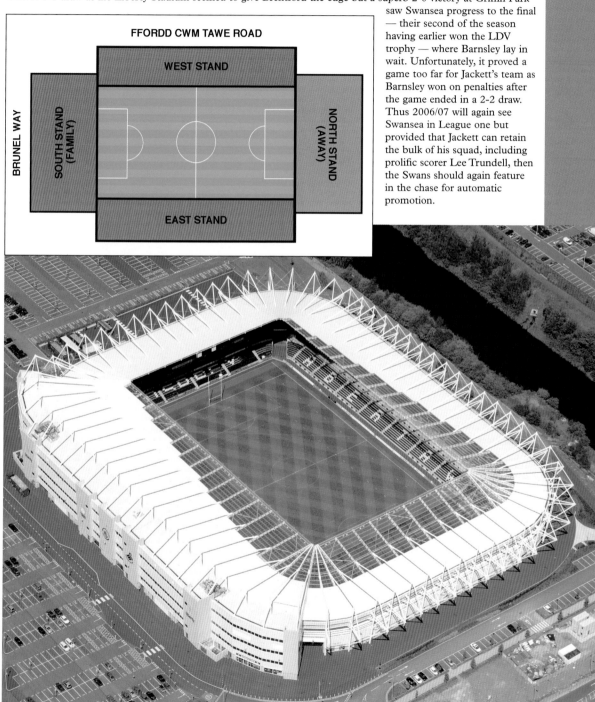

FFORDD CWM TAWE ROAD

WEST STAND

SOUTH STAND (FAMILY)

NORTH STAND (AWAY)

BRUNEL WAY

EAST STAND

County Ground, County Road, Swindon, SN1 2ED

Tel No: 0870 443 1969
Advance Tickets Tel No: 0870 443 1894
Fax: 01793 333703
Web Site: www.swindontownfc.premiumtv.co.uk
E-Mail: enquiries@swindontownfc.co.uk
League: League Two
Last Season: 23rd (relegated) in League One
(P 46; W 11; D 15; L 24; GF 46; GA 65)
Nickname: The Robins
Brief History: Founded 1881. Former
Grounds: Quarry Ground, Globe Road, Croft
Ground, County Ground (adjacent to current
Ground and now Cricket Ground), moved to
current County Ground in 1896. Founder-
members Third Division (1920). Record
attendance 32,000
(Total) Current Capacity: 15,700 (all seated)
Visiting Supporters' Allocation: 3,342 (all
seated) in Arkell's Stand and Stratton Bank
(open)

Club Colours: Red shirts, white shorts
Nearest Railway Station: Swindon
Parking (Car): Town Centre
Parking (Coach/Bus): Adjacent car park
Police Force and Tel No: Wiltshire (01793
528111)
Disabled Visitors' Facilities:
Wheelchairs: In front of Arkell's Stand
Blind: Commentary available
Anticipated Development(s): The proposed
relocation to the west of the town, at Shaw Tip,
was thwarted in July 2004 when the local
council decided not to sacrifice the community
forest located at the site. The failure of the
proposed move, which had been opposed by
residents and many fans, resulted in the club
seeking planning permission to redevelop its
existing ground in February 2005.

SWINDON TOWN

KEY
C Club Offices
S Club Shop
E Entrance(s) for visiting
supporters

↑ North direction (approx)

❶ Shrivenham Road
❷ Stratton Bank (away)
❸ A345 Queens Drive (M4
Junction 15 – 3½ miles)
❹ Swindon BR Station (½ mile)
❺ Town End
❻ Car Park
❼ County Cricket Ground
❽ Nationwide Stand
❾ Arkell's Stand
❿ 'Magic' Roundabout

Above: 699231; *Right:* 699234

COUNTY ROAD

TOWN END
(OVERFLOW)

ARKELLS STAND

| AR1 | FAM | AR3 | AR4 | AWAY |
| KIDS | AR2 | ENCLOSURE | | |

DISABLED FANS

PITCH SIZE
114 X 74 yards

DISABLED FANS

ENCLOSURE

SOUTH STAND

| NW6 | NW5 | NW4 | NW3 | NW2 | NW1 |

SHRIVENHAM ROAD

STRATTON BANK STAND
(OPEN STAND)

AWAY

At the end of September, following a five-game run of defeats culminating in a 3-2 reverse against Bradford City that left Town in 23rd position, Andy King's five-year reign at the County Ground was brought to an end. Coach Iffy Onoura was appointed caretaker but under his control the club never really made progress on the field and relegation was confirmed before the final weekend of the season. Even in cup competitions the Robins struggled, losing to League Two opposition in both the Carling Cup (Wycombe winning 3-1 at the County Ground) and FA Cup (Boston winning 4-1 after a draw at the County Ground). After the end of the season it was confirmed that Onoura was to be replaced as manager by ex-Millwall manager Dennis Wise with Gustavo Poyet as his assistant. As a relegated team, the Robins should have the potential to be amongst the divisional pace-makers but it may well be tight between automatic promotion and the Play-Offs.

Plainmoor Ground, Torquay, TQ1 3PS

Tel No: 01803 328666
Advance Tickets Tel No: 01803 328666
Fax: 01803 323976
Web Site: www.torquayunited.premiumtv.co.uk
E-Mail: gullsfc@aol.com
League: League Two
Last Season: 20th (P 46; W 13; D 13; L 20; GF 53; GA 66)
Nickname: The Gulls
Brief History: Founded 1898, as Torquay United, amalgamated with Ellacombe in 1910, changed name to Torquay Town. Amalgamated with Babbacombe in 1921, changed name to Torquay United. Former Grounds: Teignmouth Road, Torquay Recreation Ground, Cricketfield Road & Torquay Cricket Ground, moved to Plainmoor (Ellacombe Ground) in 1910. Record attendance 21,908
(Total) Current Capacity: 6,283 (2,446 seated)

Visiting Supporters' Allocation: 1,004 (plus 196 seated in Main Stand)
Club Colours: Yellow with white stripe shirts, yellow shorts
Nearest Railway Station: Torquay (2 miles)
Parking (Car): Street parking
Parking (Coach/Bus): Lymington Road coach station
Police Force and Tel No: Devon & Cornwall (01803 214491)
Disabled Visitors' Facilities:
  Wheelchairs: Ellacombe End
  Blind: Commentary available
Anticipated Development(s): There are proposals for a joint project with a local school for the rebuilding of the Main Stand. This would give United a 2,500-seat stand but there is no confirmed timescale.

TORQUAY UNITED

KEY

C Club Offices
S Club Shop
E Entrance(s) for visiting supporters
R Refreshment bars for visiting supporters
T Toilets for visiting supporters

↑ North direction (approx)

❶ Warbro Road
❷ To B3202 Marychurch Road
❸ Marnham Road
❹ To Torquay BR Station (2 miles)
❺ To A38
❻ Sparkworld End

Above: 700394; Right: 700393

Unlucky to be relegated from League One at the end of the 2004/05 season, confidence was high at Plainmoor that under Leroy Rosenior that the Gulls would make a strong push for automatic promotion. The loss of several key players, however, resulted in the team struggling in the league — despite the encouragement of good performances against Birmingham City in the FA CUP — and, following a 3-2 home defeat by Rochdale in late January which left the team in the relegation zone resulted in Rosenior leaving the club 'by mutual consent' at the end of the month. He was replaced as caretaker by ex-Exeter City boss John Cornforth who, after a couple of reasonable results, was confirmed as permanent manager until the end of the season. However, with the Gulls still struggling, Cornforth stood down in early April to be replaced by Ian Atkins; under Atkins' control, the club made a remarkable escape although survival in the league was not - again — confirmed until the end of the season. Despite a last-day 0-0 draw at home to Boston, Oxford United's defeat consigned the latter to relegation. Atkins' success, which included victory over champions-elect Carlisle United, was to bring him both the divisional manager of the month award for April and the role of Gulls' manager for the 2006/07 season.

Consolidation is perhaps Atkins' initial aim and provided that he can strengthen the squad then a mid-table position should be achievable.

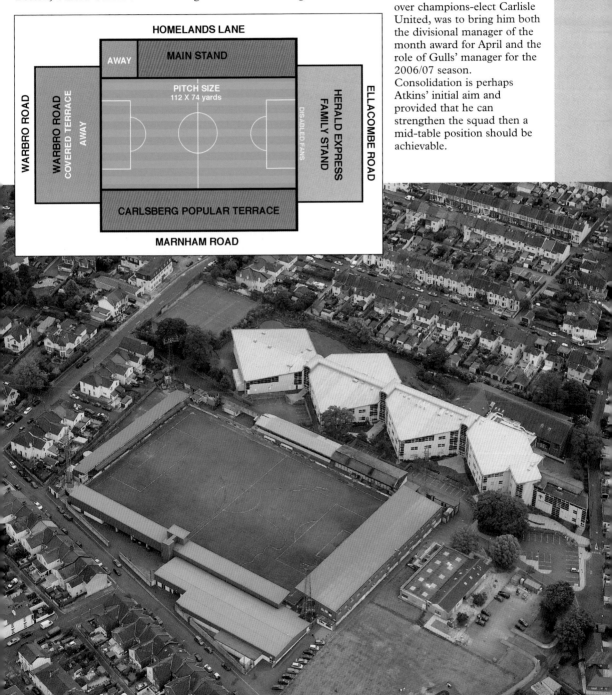

HOMELANDS LANE

AWAY

MAIN STAND

WARBRO ROAD

WARBRO ROAD COVERED TERRACE AWAY

PITCH SIZE
112 X 74 yards

DISABLED FANS

HERALD EXPRESS FAMILY STAND

ELLACOMBE ROAD

CARLSBERG POPULAR TERRACE

MARNHAM ROAD

Bill Nicholson Way, 748 High Road, Tottenham, London N17 0AP

Tel No: 0870 420 5000
Ticket Line: 0870 420 5000
Fax: 020 8365 5005
Web Site: www.tottenhamhotspur.com
E-Mail: email@tottenhamhotspur.com
League: F.A. Premier
Last Season: 5th (P38; W 18; D11; L 9; GF 53; GA 38)
Nickname: Spurs
Brief History: Founded 1882 as 'Hotspur', changed name to Tottenham Hotspur in 1885. Former Grounds: Tottenham Marshes and Northumberland Park, moved to White Hart Lane in 1899. F.A. Cup winner 1901 (as a non-League club). Record attendance 75,038
(Total) Current Capacity: 36,257 (all seated)
Visiting Supporters' Allocation: 3,000 (in South and West Stands)
Club Colours: White shirts, navy blue shorts
Nearest Railway Station: White Hart Lane plus Seven Sisters and Manor House (tube)

Parking (Car): Street parking (min ¼ mile from ground)
Parking (Coach/Bus): Northumberland Park coach park
Police Force and Tel No: Metropolitan (0208 801 3443)
Disabled Visitors' Facilities:
Wheelchairs: North and South Stands (by prior arrangement)
Blind: Commentary available
Anticipated Development(s): The local council gave permission in October 2001 for the construction of a third tier on the East Stand taking capacity to 50,000, although there is no schedule for the work and it depends on other local regeneration work. Despite the potential that this increase offers, the club is still interested ultimately in relocation.

TOTTENHAM HOTSPUR

KEY
C Club Offices
S Club Shop
E Entrance(s) for visiting supporters

↑ North direction (approx)

❶ Park Lane
❷ A1010 High Road
❸ White Hart Lane BR station
❹ Paxton Road
❺ Worcester Avenue
❻ West Stand
❼ South Stand

Above: 700261; *Right:* 700254

Under Martin Jol, Spurs had their best season in the Premier League for many years and, for much of the season, it looked as though the club would pip arch North London rivals Arsenal to the all-important fourth place and, therefore, entry into the Champions League. In the event, however, it all came down to the last day of the season; Arsenal needed to better Spurs' result if Jol's team was not to enter the elite competition. The Gunners faced Wigan at Highbury whilst Spurs took on another promoted team, West Ham, at Upton Park. Unfortunately, the Spurs' players were afflicted by an outbreak of illness, widely reported at the time to be food poisoning, and, with the club having failed in an appeal to the FA to get the game deferred or postponed, lost. At Highbury, however, Arsenal overcame spirited Wigan resistance to achieve a victory that snatched fourth place from Tottenham. However, fifth place does bring with it entry into European football, courtesy of the UEFA Cup, and, with Jol looking to strengthen the squad over the summer, there is every likelihood that Spurs will again feature in the chase for one of the Champions League places.

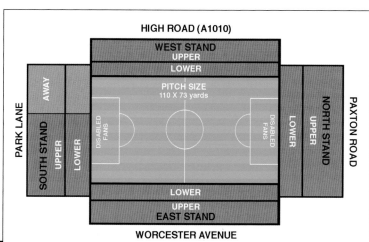

Prenton Park, Prenton Road West, Birkenhead, CH42 9PY

Tel No: 0870 460 3333
Advance Tickets Tel No: 0870 460 3332
Fax: 0151 609 0606
Web Site: www.tranmererovers.premiumtv.co.uk
E-Mail: info@tranmererovers.co.uk
League: League One
Last Season: 18th (P46; W 13; D 15; L 18; GF 50; GA 52)
Nickname: Rovers
Brief History: Founded 1884 as Belmont F.C., changed name to Tranmere Rovers in 1885 (not connected to earlier 'Tranmere Rovers'). Former grounds: Steele's Field and Ravenshaw's Field (also known as Old Prenton Park, ground of Tranmere Rugby Club), moved to (new) Prenton Park in 1911. Founder-members 3rd Division North (1921). Record attendance 24,424

(Total) Current Capacity: 16,587 (all seated)
Visiting Supporters' Allocation: 2,500 (all-seated) in Cow Shed Stand
Club Colours: White shirts, white shorts
Nearest Railway Station: Hamilton Square or Rock Ferry
Parking (Car): Car park at Ground
Parking (Coach/Bus): Car park at Ground
Police Force and Tel No: Merseyside (0151 709 6010)
Disabled Visitors' Facilities:
  Wheelchairs: Main Stand
  Blind: Commentary available

TRANMERE ROVERS

KEY

C Club Offices
S Club Shop
E Entrance(s) for visiting supporters

↑ North direction (approx)

❶ Car Park
❷ Prenton Road West
❸ Borough Road
❹ M53 Junction 4 (B5151) – 3 miles
❺ Birkenhead (1 mile)
❻ Cow Shed Stand
❼ Kop Shed

172

Above: 698977; *Right:* 698983

Following the disappointing end to the 2004/05 season when Rovers just failed to make it through the Play-Offs, expectations were high at Prenton Park that the new season would bring the club promotion. However, a disappointing campaign, which saw the team emerge as one of the division's draw specialists, saw Rovers hover just above the drop zone. Whilst the club was never actually sucked into the relegation battle, such was the tightness of League One that the club could, quite easily have been dragged into the mire if results had gone differently, and, shortly before the final game of the season, Brian Little departed as manager. He was replaced as manager for the final game of the season by Jason McAteer; his first game in charge, however, resulted in a 2-0 defeat at home by Doncaster Rovers which left Rovers in 18th place just four points above relegated Hartlepool. New manager Ronnie Moore, the ex-Rotherham and Oldham boss, will undoubtedly have to reshape the team for 2006/07 if the club is not again to face a battle at the bottom of League One; perhaps the best that fans can look forward to is a season of consolidation in mid-table with the outside possibility of the Play-Offs.

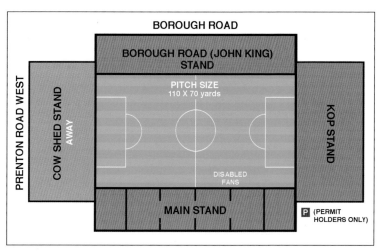

BOROUGH ROAD

BOROUGH ROAD (JOHN KING) STAND

PITCH SIZE
110 X 70 yards

PRENTON ROAD WEST

COW SHED STAND
AWAY

KOP STAND

DISABLED FANS

MAIN STAND

P (PERMIT HOLDERS ONLY)

Bescot Stadium, Bescot Crescent, Walsall, West Midlands, WS1 4SA

Tel No: 0870 442 0442
Advance Tickets Tel No: 0870 442 0111
Fax: 01922 613202
Web Site: www.saddlers.premiumtv.co.uk/
E-Mail: commercial@walsallfc.co.uk
League: League Two
Last Season: 24th (relegated) (P 46; W 11; D 14; L 21; GF 47; GA 70)
Nickname: The Saddlers
Brief History: Founded 1888 as Walsall Town Swifts (amalgamation of Walsall Town – founded 1884 – and Walsall Swifts – founded 1885), changed name to Walsall in 1895. Former Grounds: The Chuckery, West Bromwich Road (twice), Hilary Street (later named Fellows Park, twice), moved to Bescot Stadium in 1990. Founder-members Second Division (1892). Record attendance 10,628 (25,343 at Fellows Park)
(Total) Current Capacity: 11,300 (all seated)

Visiting Supporters' Allocation: 2,000 maximum in William Sharp Stand
Club Colours: Red shirts, red shorts
Nearest Railway Station: Bescot
Parking (Car): Car park at Ground
Parking (Coach/Bus): Car park at Ground
Police Force and Tel No: West Midlands (01922 638111)
Disabled Visitors' Facilities:
Wheelchairs: Bank's Stand
Blind: No special facility
Anticipated Development(s): Planning permission was granted in the summer of 2004 for the redevelopment of the William Sharp Stand to add a further 2,300 seats, taking the away allocation up to 4,000 and the total ground capacity to 13,500. The project is to be funded via advertising directed towards the adjacent M6 but work has yet to commence.

KEY

C Club Offices
S Club Shop
E Entrance(s) for visiting supporters

⬆ North direction (approx)

❶ Motorway M6
❷ M6 Junction 9
❸ Bescot BR Station
❹ Car Parks
❺ Bescot Crescent
❻ Gilbert Alsop Stand
❼ William Sharp Stand

WALSALL

174

Above: 699950; *Right:* 699960

In early February, following a disappointing run of results culminating in a 5-0 defeat at high-flying Brentford which left the Saddlers one point clear of the relegation zone, Paul Merson was sacked as boss after almost two years in the job. Mick Halsall took over as caretaker until the club appointed ex-Northampton boss Kevan Broadhurst as manager initially until the end of the season. Unfortunately, unlike Nottingham Forest and Bristol City, where a change of manager resulted in a dramatic improvement in fortunes, for the Saddlers there was no change and a home defeat against Huddersfield resulted in the team's relegation. It was then announced that Broadhurst had been sacked with Mark Kinsella taking over for the final two games of the season. As one of the relegated teams, Walsall will fancy their chances of making an immediate return to League One but new boss Richard Money will perhaps struggle to make the Play-Offs at best.

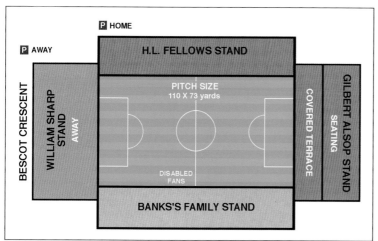

P HOME

P AWAY

H.L. FELLOWS STAND

BESCOT CRESCENT

WILLIAM SHARP STAND

AWAY

PITCH SIZE
110 X 73 yards

DISABLED FANS

COVERED TERRACE

GILBERT ALSOP STAND

SEATING

BANKS'S FAMILY STAND

Vicarage Road Stadium, Vicarage Road, Watford, WD18 0ER

Tel No: 0870 111 1881
Advance Tickets Tel No: 0870 111 1881
Fax: 01923 496001
Web Site: www.watfordfc.premiumtv.co.uk
E-Mail: yourvoice@watfordfc.com
League: F.A. Premier
Last Season: 3rd (promoted via the Play-Offs) (P 46; W 22; D 15; L 9; GF 77; GA 53)
Nickname: The Hornets
Brief History: Founded 1898 as an amalgamation of West Herts (founded 1891) and Watford St. Mary's (founded early 1890s). Former Grounds: Wiggenhall Road (Watford St. Mary's) and West Herts Sports Ground, moved to Vicarage Road in 1922. Founder-members Third Division (1920). Record attendance 34,099
(Total) Current Capacity: 20,250 (all seated)
Visiting Supporters' Allocation: 4,500 maximum in Vicarage Road (North) Stand
Club Colours: Yellow shirts, red shorts
Nearest Railway Station: Watford High Street or Watford Junction
Parking (Car): Nearby multi-storey car park in town centre (10 mins walk)
Parking (Coach/Bus): Cardiff Road car park
Other Clubs Sharing Ground: Saracens RUFC
Police Force and Tel No: Hertfordshire (01923 472000)
Disabled Visitors' Facilities:
  Wheelchairs: Corner East Stand and South Stand (special enclosure for approx. 24 wheelchairs), plus enclosure in North East Corner
  Blind: Commentary available in the East Stand (20 seats, free of charge)
Anticipated Development(s): The club's plans for the reconstruction of the East Stand are still in abeyance. However, as a result of safety concerns, part of the existing structure was closed during the close season of 2004, reducing the ground's capacity. This necessitated relocating some 600 season ticket holders as well as the board and press box. The plans for the new stand, for which there remains no definite timescale, anticipate the construction of a new 4,500-seat structure, taking Watford's capacity to 23,000.

KEY

C Club Offices
S Club Shop

↑ North direction (approx)

❶ Vicarage Road
❷ Occupation Road
❸ Rous Stand
❹ Town Centre (1/2 mile) – Car Parks, High Street BR Station
❺ Vicarage Road Stand (away)
❻ East Stand
❼ Rookery End

WATFORD

Above: 699838; *Right:* 699842

Widely perceived as almost certain candidates for automatic relegation, Adrian Boothroyd's team confounded the critics and found itself in the Play-Off positions virtually throughout the campaign. Whilst never strong enough to threaten one of the top two spots — despite Sheffield United's blip in form in the middle of the season — the Hornets secured third place and a spot in the Play-Offs. Victory in the semi-finals over a lacklustre Crystal Palace set up a Millennium Stadium encounter with Leeds United. Historically, teams that finish third have often failed at this last stage, but on this occasion Watford proved too strong for Leeds, winning comfortably 3-0. Thus, after a gap of six years, the Hornets return to the top flight. When last there, in 1999/2000, the team lasted a single season and achieved a then record low in terms of points scored. Given the record low that Sunderland achieved in 20056/06, it's hard to see Watford doing quite as badly in 2006/07 but it's also difficult to escape the conclusion that fans of the Hornets should enjoy their season in the Premier League as, in 2007/08, the team's likely to be back in the Championship.

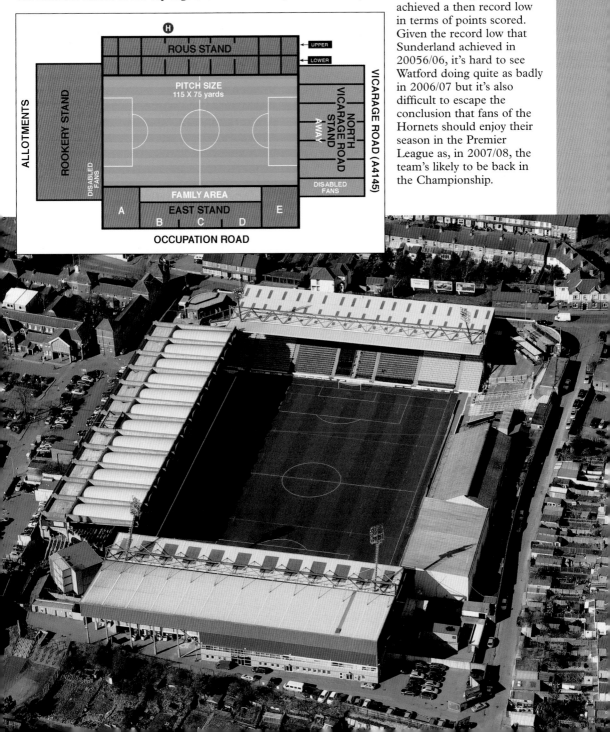

The Hawthorns, Halfords Lane, West Bromwich, West Midlands, B71 4LF

Tel No: 08700 668888
Advance Tickets Tel No: 08700 662800
Fax: 08700 662861
Web Site: www.wba.premiumtv.co.uk
E-Mail: enquiries@wbafc.co.uk
League: League Championship
Last Season: 19th (relegated) (P 38; W 7; D 9; L 22; GF 31; GA 58)
Nickname: The Baggies
Brief History: Founded 1879. Former Grounds: Coopers Hill, Dartmouth Park, Four Acres, Stoney Lane, moved to the Hawthorns in 1900. Founder-members of Football League (1888). Record attendance 64,815
(Total) Current Capacity: 28,000 (all seated)
Visiting Supporters' Allocation: 3,000 in Smethwick End (can be increased to 5,200 if required)

Club Colours: Navy blue and white striped shirts, white shorts
Nearest Railway Station: The Hawthorns
Parking (Car): Halfords Lane and Rainbow Stand car parks
Parking (Coach/Bus): Rainbow Stand car park
Police Force and Tel No: West Midlands (0121 554 3414)
Disabled Visitors' Facilities:
  Wheelchairs: Apollo 2000 and Smethwick Road End
  Blind: Facility available
Anticipated Development(s): There is speculation that the club will seek to increase capacity to 30,000 by rebuilding the area between the Apollo and East stands, but nothing is confirmed.

KEY

C Club Offices
S Club Shop
E Entrance(s) for visiting supporters

↑ North direction (approx)

❶ A41 Birmingham Road
❷ To M5 Junction 1
❸ Birmingham Centre (4 miles)
❹ Halfords Lane
❺ Main Stand
❻ Smethwick End
❼ Rolfe Street, Smethwick BR Station (1½ miles)
❽ To The Hawthorns BR Station
❾ East (Rainbow) Stand
❿ Apollo 2000 Stand

Above: 699262; *Right:* 699266

Following the great escape at the end of the 2004/05 season, when the Baggies were the first team in the Premier League to escape the 'last at Christmas' curse, there was considerable confidence at The Hawthorns that, in 2005/06, the team would not face the same struggle to retain its Premier League status. After all, there was a pretty widespread view that Wigan was simply in the division to make up the numbers and the other promoted clubs were not considered particularly strong; in the event, however, whilst Sunderland lived down to these expectations, both Wigan and West Ham prospered and West Brom found itself embroiled for most of the campaign battling against the drop. For fans, however, there was to be no last day drama this season as, by the last Sunday of the campaign, the team was already relegated, sunk by a dramatic improvement in the fortunes of Portsmouth and Pompey's away victory at Wigan the previous week. The last time a Bryan Robson-managed team was relegated — Middlesbrough — the club made an immediate return, as did the Baggies when last relegated; however, the League Championship looks stronger in 2006/07 and West Brom will only prosper in they can retain as many of their quality players. The Baggies should be in the mix for promotion or the Play-Offs, but as both Norwich and Southampton discovered in 2005/06, the Championship can be a harsh environment for relegated teams.

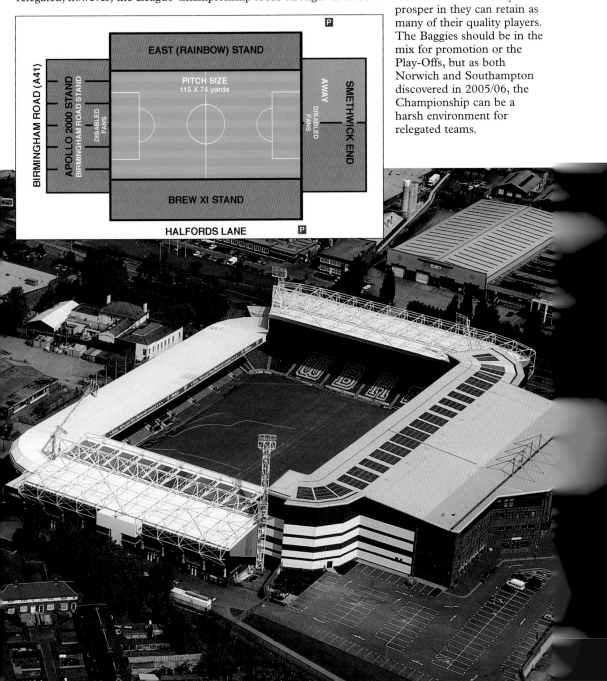

Boleyn Ground, Green Street, Upton Park, London, E13 9AZ

Tel No: 020 8548 2748
Advance Tickets Tel No: 0870 112 2700
Fax: 020 8548 2758
Web Site: www.whufc.co.uk
E-Mail: yourcomments@westhamunited.co.uk
League: F.A. Premier
Last Season: 9th (P 38; W 16; D 7; L 15; GF 52; GA 55)
Nickname: The Hammers
Brief History: Founded 1895 as Thames Ironworks, changed name to West Ham United in 1900. Former Grounds: Hermit Road, Browning Road, The Memorial Ground, moved to Boleyn Ground in 1904. Record attendance 42,322
(Total) Current Capacity: 35,647 (all seated)
Visiting Supporters' Allocation: 3,700 maximum
Club Colours: Claret and blue shirts, white shorts

Nearest Railway Station: Barking BR, Upton Park (tube)
Parking (Car): Street parking
Parking (Coach/Bus): As directed by Police
Police Force and Tel No: Metropolitan (020 8593 8232)
Disabled Visitors' Facilities:
  Wheelchairs: West Lower, Bobby Moore and Centenary Stands
  Blind: Commentaries available
Anticipated Development(s): With the Stratford area due to receive massive investment as a result of London's victory in obtaining the 2012 Olympics, the possibility of West Ham United moving to the Olympic Stadium after the games has been raised. Nothing, however, has been confirmed at this stage.

WEST HAM UNITED

KEY

E Entrance(s) for visiting supporters

⬆ North direction (approx)

❶ A124 Barking Road
❷ Green Street
❸ North Stand
❹ Upton Park Tube Station (¼ mile)
❺ Barking BR Station (1 mile)
❻ Bobby Moore Stand
❼ East Stand
❽ West Stand

Above: 699352; Right: 699342

Promoted at the end of the 2004/05 season through the Play-Offs, most pundits had inked West Ham in as almost certain candidates for an immediate return to the League Championship. As with Wigan, however, the pundits were to be proved wrong as Alan Pardew's side the Hammers were ultimately to achieve an impressive ninth place in the League and also an FA Cup Final appearance against Liverpool at the Millennium Stadium. In one of the greatest Cup Finals of all time, the Hammers led for most of the game before a Steven Gerrard equaliser in the first minute in injury time. With no further goals in extra time, the game went to penalties and, unfortunately for fans of the Hammers, the London team lost. Although defeated, Liverpool's involvement in the Champions League guaranteed West Ham a place in the 2006/07 UEFA Cup. As other teams have found in the past, the second season in the Premier League can sometimes prove more difficult than the first and, as Ipswich discovered some years ago, involvement in European competition can sometimes prove to be a distraction. Given the apparent weakness of the three promoted teams, the Hammers ought to be able to cement their Premier League status again with ease but injuries or loss of confidence could prove telling.

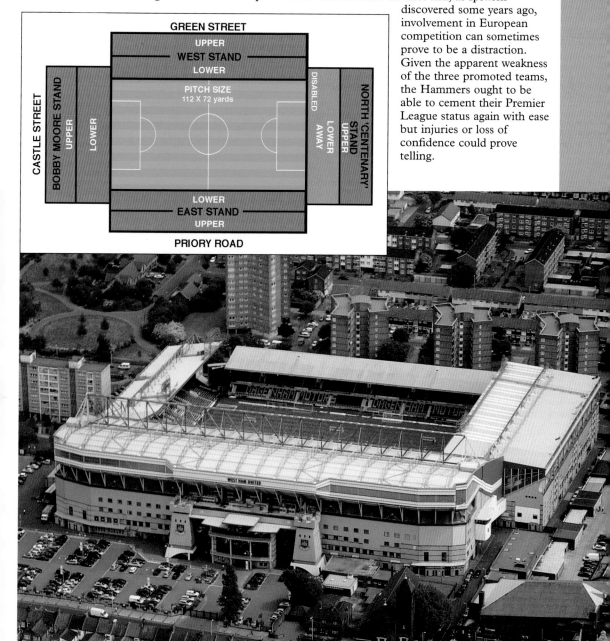

Tel No: 01942 774000
Advance Tickets Tel No: 0870 112 2552
Fax: 01942 770477
Web Site: www.wiganlatics.premiumtv.co.uk
E-Mail: s.hayton@jjbstadium.co.uk
League: F.A. Premier
Last Season: 10th (P 38; W 15; D 6; L 17; GF 45; GA 52)
Nickname: The Latics
Brief History: Founded 1932. Springfield Park used by former Wigan Borough (Football League 1921-1931) but unrelated to current club. Elected to Football League in 1978 (the last club to be elected rather than promoted). Moved to JJB Stadium for start of 1999/2000 season. Record attendance at Springfield Park 27,500; at JJB Stadium 25,015
(Total) Current Capacity: 25,000 (all-seated)
Visiting Supporters' Allocation: 8,178 (maximum) in East (Adidas) Stand (all-seated)

Club Colours: White and blue shirts, blue shorts
Nearest Railway Stations: Wigan Wallgate/Wigan North Western (both about 1.5 miles away)
Parking (Car): 2,500 spaces at the ground
Parking (Coach/Bus): As directed
Other Clubs Sharing Ground: Wigan Warriors RLFC
Police Force and Tel No: Greater Manchester (0161 872 5050)
Disabled Visitors' Facilities
  Wheelchairs: 100 spaces
  Blind: No special facility although it is hoped to have a system in place shortly
Anticipated Development(s): None following completion of the ground.

KEY

C Club Offices
E Entrance(s) for visiting supporters

↑ North direction (approx)

❶ Loire Drive
❷ Anjoy Boulevard
❸ Car Parks
❹ Robin Park Arena
❺ River Douglas
❻ Leeds-Liverpool Canal
❼ To A577/A49 and Wigan town centre plus Wigan (Wallgate) and Wigan (North Western) station
❽ East Stand
❾ South Stand
❿ North Stand
⓫ West Stand

Above: 699269; *Right:* 699272

WIGAN ATHLETIC

Widely considered before the start of the 2005/06 to be the Premier League's whipping boys, the Latics proved most pundits wrong in that, not only did they prosper rather than struggle to survive in the division, they also were outside bets for a European place right up until the end of the season. In Paul Jewell the club was fortunate to possess a manager who was experienced at managing an unfancied team in the Premier League and whose acquisitions proved astute in keeping the team moving forward even during those periods when the results were not going in the team's favour. However, the problem in 2006/07 may well be to repeat the trick; there have been a number of clubs in recent years that have survived the first season only to find the second a struggle — most recently West Brom who went down at the end of the 2005/06 season — and whether or not Wigan face the same tribulations will depend to a significant extent on how many of his squad Jewell can retain and the quality of those players that he can recruit. Already there are signs that a number of players — such as Bullard — are already on their way out from the JJB Stadium.

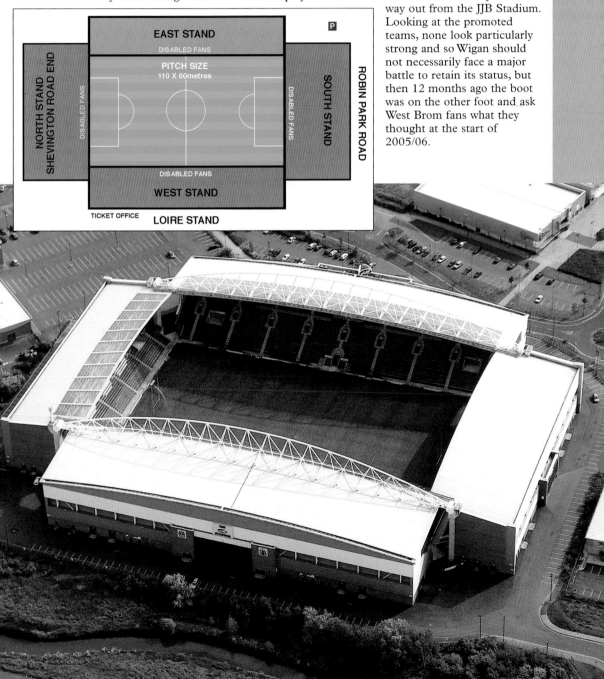

Looking at the promoted teams, none look particularly strong and so Wigan should not necessarily face a major battle to retain its status, but then 12 months ago the boot was on the other foot and ask West Brom fans what they thought at the start of 2005/06.

Molineux Ground, Waterloo Road, Wolverhampton, WV1 4QR

Tel No: 0870 442 0123
Advance Tickets Tel No: 0870 442 0123
Fax: 01902 687006
Web Site: www.wolves.premiumtv.co.uk
E-Mail: info@wolves.co.uk
League: League Championship
Last Season: 7th (P 46; W 16; D 19; L 11; GF 50; GA 42)
Nickname: Wolves
Brief History: Founded 1877 as St. Lukes, combined with Goldthorn Hill to become Wolverhampton Wanderers in 1884. Former Grounds: Old Windmill Field, John Harper's Field and Dudley Road, moved to Molineux in 1889. Founder-members Football League (1888). Record attendance 61,315
(Total) Current Capacity: 29,400 (all seated)
Visiting Supporters' Allocation: 3,200 in lower tier of Steve Bull Stand or 2,000 in Jack Harris Stand
Club Colours: Gold shirts, black shorts

Nearest Railway Station: Wolverhampton
Parking (Car): West Park and adjacent North Bank
Parking (Coach/Bus): As directed by Police
Police Force and Tel No: West Midlands (01902 649000)
Disabled Visitors' Facilities:
 Wheelchairs: 104 places on two sides
 Blind: Commentary (by prior arrangement)
Anticipated Developments: The club installed some 900 seats on a temporary stand between the Billy Wright and Jack Harris stands for the season in the Premiership. The club has plans to expand the capacity of Molineux to more than 40,000 by adding second tiers to the Stan Cullis and Jack Harris stands and completely rebuilding the Steve Bull Stand. There is no timescale for the work but it is unlikely to proceed until the club regains (and retains) a place in the Premiership.

KEY

C Club Offices
S Club Shop
E Entrance(s) for visiting supporters
R Refreshment bars for visiting supporters
T Toilets for visiting supporters

↑ North direction (approx)

❶ Stan Cullis Stand
❷ Steve Bull Stand
❸ Billy Wright Stand
❹ Ring Road – St. Peters
❺ Waterloo Road
❻ A449 Stafford Street
❼ BR Station (½ mile)
❽ Jack Harris Stand
❾ Molineux Street
❿ Molineux Way
⓫ Temporary additional seating

Above: 696908; *Right:* 696013

A frustrating season at Molyneux saw Wolves in the hunt for the Play-Offs throughout the campaign but never actually sustain a challenge for long enough ever to threaten seriously a top-six finish. As the Championship's draw specialists, Wolves drew no fewer than 19 times during the season, including 10 games at home, and ultimately it was the team's failure to convert these single point matches into victories that was to cost them dear. Towards the end of the season, as the club's Play-Off hopes faded, the position of manager Glenn Hoddle came increasingly into focus. Although, Hoddle's position for the 2006/07 season was confirmed he subsequently decided to resign and was replaced by Mick McCarthy. Wolves undoubtedly has the potential to make a more sustained challenge in 2006/07 but the Play-Offs may again be the club's best hope of a return to the Premier League.

WOLVERHAMPTON RING ROAD

WATERLOO ROAD

OPEN SEATING

BILLY WRIGHT STAND

PITCH SIZE
116 X 74 yards

JACK HARRIS STAND

DISABLED

STAN CULLIS STAND

DISABLED

AWAY LOWER TIER

UPPER TIER
STEVE BULL STAND

MOLINEUX STAND

Racecourse Ground, Mold Road, Wrexham, Clwyd LL11 2AH

Tel No: 01978 262129
Advance Tickets Tel No: 01978 262129
Web Site: www.wrexhamafc.premiumtv.co.uk
E-Mail: geraint@wrexhamfc.co.uk
Fax: 01978 357821
League: League Two
Last season: 13th (P46; W 15; D 14; L 17; GF 61; GA 54)
Nickname: The Red Dragons or the Robins
Brief History: Founded 1873 (oldest Football Club in Wales). Former Ground: Acton Park, permanent move to Racecourse Ground c.1900. Founder-members Third Division North (1921). Record attendance 34,445
(Total) Current Capacity: 15,500 (11,500 seated)
Visiting Supporters' Allocation: 3,100 (maximum; all seated)
Club Colours: Red shirts, white shorts

Nearest Railway Station: Wrexham General
Parking (Car): (Nearby) Town car parks
Parking (Coach/Bus): As directed by Police
Police Force and Tel No: Wrexham Division (01978 290222)
Disabled Visitors' Facilities:
  Wheelchairs: Pryce Griffiths Stand
  Blind: No special facility
Anticipated Development(s): As part of the deal that saw the club move towards an exit from administration, the club announced in early June that it intended to redevelop the Crispin Lane (Kop) End of the ground. A new stand would be constructed along with flats and a 500sq m retail space. At the time of writing there was no formal permission for the work had been sought from the council nor was there a confirmed timescale for the work to be undertaken.

KEY

C Club Offices
S Club Shop
E Entrance(s) for visiting supporters
R Refreshment bars for visiting supporters
T Toilets for visiting supporters

⬆ North direction (approx)

❶ Wrexham General Station
❷ A541 – Mold Road
❸ Wrexham Town Centre
❹ Pryce Griffiths Stand
❺ Kop Town End
❻ To Wrexham Central Station
❼ Roberts Builders Stand (away)

Above: 700003; *Right:* 700007

WREXHAM

Relegated at the end of the 2004/05 season as the first team to be docked 10 points as a result of going into Administration, the primary concern of the Wrexham faithful during the close season was to ensure that they had a team to support during 2005/06. The fact that the players ultimately finished in 13th position was overshadowed by concerns that the club could be expelled by the Football League after the end of the season for having been in Administration for 18 months. In the event, a rescue plan to take the club out of Administration was accepted by the Football League in early June ensuring that the Red Dragons could continue in League Two for the 2006/07 season. With uncertainty over the club's future largely removed Denis Smith should be able to use the close season to develop further his squad and, using the 13th place achieved at the end of a difficult season as a foundation, build for the new season with every expectation of being able to challenge for the Play-Offs.

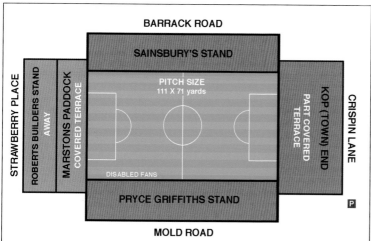

BARRACK ROAD

SAINSBURY'S STAND

STRAWBERRY PLACE

ROBERTS BUILDERS STAND
AWAY

MARSTONS PADDOCK
COVERED TERRACE

PITCH SIZE
111 X 71 yards

DISABLED FANS

KOP (TOWN) END
PART COVERED
TERRACE

CRISPIN LANE

PRYCE GRIFFITHS STAND

P

MOLD ROAD

Adams Park, Hillbottom Road, Sands, High Wycombe, Bucks HP12 4HJ

Tel No: 01494 472100
Advance Tickets Tel No: 01494 441118
Fax: 01494 527633
Web Site: www.wycombewanderers.premiumtv.co.uk
E-Mail: wwfc@wwfc.com
League: League Two
Last season: 15th (P46; W 15; D 11; L 20; GF 54; GA 62)
Nickname: The Chairboys
Brief History: Founded 1884. Former Grounds: The Rye, Spring Meadows, Loakes Park, moved to Adams Park 1990. Promoted to Football League 1993. Record attendance 15,678 (Loakes Park); 9,921 (Adams Park)
(Total) Current Capacity: 10,000 (8,250 seated)
Visiting Supporters' Allocation: c2,000 in the Roger Vere Stand
Club Colours: Sky blue with navy blue quartered shirts, blue shorts

Nearest Railway Station: High Wycombe (2½ miles)
Parking (Car): At Ground and Street parking
Parking (Coach/Bus): At Ground
Other Clubs Sharing Ground: London Wasps RUFC
Police Force and Tel No: Thames Valley (01494 465888)
Disabled Visitors' Facilities:
　Wheelchairs: Special shelter – Main Stand, Hillbottom Road end
　Blind: Commentary available
Anticipated Development(s): The club has tentative plans to increase the ground's capacity to some 12-15,000 through the redevelopment of the Main Stand. There is, however, no timescale for this work, a project that would also require the construction of a new access road.

KEY
C Club Offices
S Club Shop
E Entrance(s) for visiting supporters

⬆ North direction (approx)

❶ Car Park
❷ Hillbottom Road (Industrial Estate)
❸ M40 Junction 4 (approx 2 miles)
❹ Wycombe Town Centre (approx 2¹/₂ miles)
❺ Woodlands Stand
❻ Roger Vere Stand (away)
❼ Syan Stand
❽ Amersham & Wycombe College Stand

Above: 699217; *Right:* 699226

A season of considerable disappointment and sadness both on and off the pitch at Adams Park saw the Chairboys ultimately fail in their quest to escape from League Two. For the first part of the season, however, it appeared that the team could do no wrong — the club possessed the longest unbeaten run of any team in the top four divisions extending to more than 20 games and had a good 3-1 win at Swindon Town in the first round of the Carling cup — and that automatic promotion was all but a certainty. The second half of the campaign was less successful and ultimately the club had to settle for a place in the Play-Offs. Unfortunately defeat over two legs by Cheltenham meant that League Two football will again be on offer in 2006/07. However, events on the field were overshadowed by events off it; in January, promising midfield Mark Philo was killed in a road accident and, later in the season, manager John Gorman was given compassionate leave as he tended his dying wife. In the event, with the season completed, it was announced that Gorman would not be returning to the club, to his disappointment. New manager — Paul Lambert — will have his work cut out to restore morale in the team and, perhaps, the Play-Offs are again the best that the fans can expect during the new season.

WOODLANDS STAND
UPPER TIER
HYPNOS FAMILY ENCLOSURE
PITCH SIZE
115 X 75 yards
THE ROGER VERE STAND
AWAY
SYAN STAND
(HOME TERRACE ONLY)
PART COVERED
AWAY FANS BLOCKS V & H
AMERSHAM & WYCOMBE COLLEGE STAND
P

Huish Park, Lufton Way, Yeovil, Somerset BA22 8YF

Tel No: 01935 423662
Advance Tickets Tel No: 01935 423662
Fax: 01935 473956
Web Site: www.ytfc.premiumtv.co.uk
E-Mail: media@ytfc.net
League League One
Last season: 15th (P46; W 15; D 11; L 20;
GF 54; GA 62)
Nickname: The Glovers
Brief History: Founded as Yeovil Casuals in
1895 and merged with Petters United in 1920.
Moved to old ground (Huish) in 1920 and
relocated to Huish Park in 1990. Founder
members of Alliance Premier League in 1979
but relegated in 1985. Returned to Premier
League in 1988 but again relegated in 1996.
Promoted to the now retitled Conference in
1997 and promoted to the Nationwide League
in 2003. Record Attendance: (at Huish)
16,318 (at Huish Park) 9,348

(Total) Current Capacity: 9,400 (5,212
seated)
Visiting Supporters' Allocation: 1,700 on
Copse Road Terrace (open) plus c400 seats in
Bartlett Stand.
Club Colours: Green shirts, white shorts
Nearest Railway Station: Yeovil Junction or
Yeovil Pen Mill
Parking (Car): Car park near to stadium for
800 cars
Parking (Coach/Bus): As directed
Police Force and Tel No: Avon & Somerset
(01935 415291)
Disabled Visitors' Facilities:
  Wheelchairs: Up to 20 dedicated located in
  the Bartlett Stand
  Blind: No special facility

KEY

⬆ North direction (approx)

❶ Western Avenue
❷ Copse Road
❸ Lufton Way
❹ Artillery Road
❺ Main (Yeovil College) Stand
❻ Bartlett Stand
❼ Westland Stand
❽ Copse Road Terrace (away)
❾ Memorial Road
❿ Mead Avenue
⓫ To town centre (one mile)
and stations (two to four
miles)

Above: 695579; *Right:* 695573

In late September, Gary Johnson, who had been manager at Yeovil since June 2001 (making him the 12th longest serving manager at the time), announced his departure to take over the reins at Bristol City. He was replaced as caretaker by Steve Thompson who was later to be confirmed as manager until the end of the season. Under Thompson's care the club managed to stay above the relegation zone — just — although there were concerns that the club could get sucked into the drop zone when teams like Milton Keynes Dons started to put together a decent run of form towards the end of the season. In the end the team finished a creditable 15th some six points above relegated Hartlepool. One high point of the season was the 2-0 victory away at Ipswich Town in the first round of the Carling Cup. In early June it was announced that Russell Slade, who'd just left Grimsby Town, would be taking over as manager with Thompson remaining as his assistant. Slade is well experienced at this level and should be capable of cementing further the Glovers' League One status. Whilst probably not being good enough for the Play-Offs, the team should probably improve on 15th in 2006/07 and perhaps achieve a top half finish.

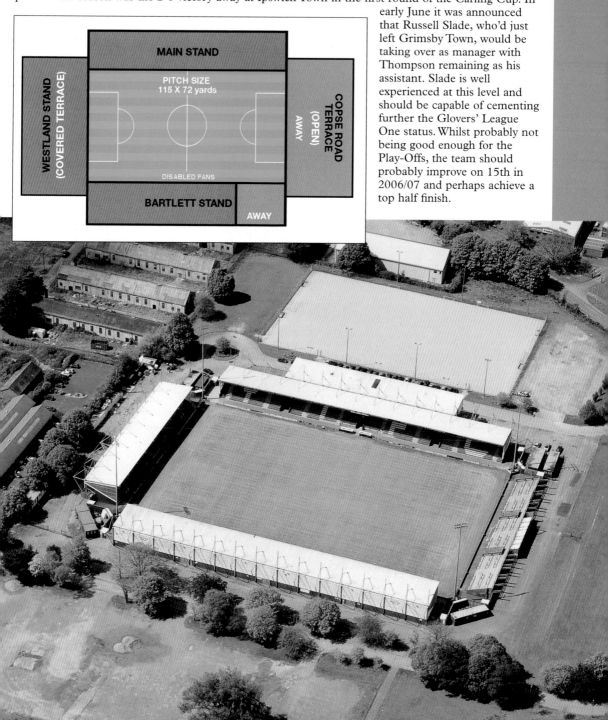

MAIN STAND

PITCH SIZE
115 X 72 yards

WESTLAND STAND
(COVERED TERRACE)

COPSE ROAD
TERRACE
(OPEN)

AWAY

DISABLED FANS

BARTLETT STAND

AWAY

Wembley Stadium, Wembley HA9 0DW

Tel No: tbc

Advance Tickets Tel No: tbc

Fax: tbc

Brief History: Inaugurated for FA Cup Final of 1923, venue for many major national and international matches including the World Cup Final of 1966. Also traditionally used for other major sporting events and as a venue for rock concerts and other entertainments. Last used prior to redevelopment as a football ground versus Germany in October 2001. Ground subsequently demolished during late 2002.

(Total) Current Capacity: tbc

Nearest Railway Station: Wembley Complex (National Rail), Wembley Central (National Rail and London Underground), Wembley Park (London Underground)

Parking (Car): Limited parking at ground and nearby

Parking (Coach Bus): As advised by police

Police Force: Metropolitan

Disabled Facilities

Wheelchairs: tbc

Blind: tbc

Anticipated Development(s): After several years of dithering and following the final game played at the 'old' Wembley, demolition of the old ground was completed in late 2002 and work started on the construction of the new stadium. This was scheduled for completion in 2006 but it is now hoped that the completed ground will host the 2007 FA Cup Final.

WEMBLEY

Above: 700265